You Can Write Better English

Barry Kalb

Journalism and
The University o
香港大學新聞
http://jmsc.hk

D1738724

in association

香港大學出版社
HONG KONG UNIVERSITY PRESS

Journalism and Media Studies Centre

G24 Eliot Hall
The University of Hong Kong
Pokfulam Road, Hong Kong
Tel: (852) 2859-1155
Fax: (852) 2858-8736
E-mail: jmsc@hku.hk
http://jmsc.hku.hk/

Author: Barry Kalb

Published by Journalism and Media Studies Centre,
The University of Hong Kong

Distributed by Hong Kong University Press

14/F Hing Wai Centre
7 Tin Wan Praya Road
Aberdeen, Hong Kong
Tel: (852) 2550-2703
Fax: (852) 2875-0734
E-mail: hkupress@hku.hk
www.hkupress.org

© Journalism and Media Studies Centre 2010
First published 2010
Reprinted 2010

ISBN 978-988-19460-1-0

Designed by Matthew Leung, Journalism and Media Studies Centre

You *Can* Write Better English

Barry Kalb

A practical handbook to help improve written English, with special focus on mistakes native Chinese speakers routinely make when writing in the English language

INTRODUCTION

The most important language skill in the professional world today is good written English.

That's what researchers at Hong Kong Polytechnic University learned from a study they conducted in 2008.

Their conclusion would be no surprise if the study had been conducted in the United States or Britain, but the people questioned for this study were professionals living and working in Hong Kong.

In the Hong Kong workplace, these professionals said, written English is more important than spoken Cantonese, more important than spoken Putonghua, more important than written Chinese.

Why is this so? Why should it be so urgent for young professionals in Hong Kong, or Mainland China or Taiwan, to be able to write good English?

The answer is simple. English is the language of international commerce and communication. People doing business between China and Chile, or Japan and Germany, or South Korea and South Africa, are more likely to conduct that business in English than in any other language.

Employers realize this, and partly as a result, a degree from a good university is no longer enough to guarantee a good job. There are hundreds of thousands of university graduates at any time competing for a limited number of jobs in the Greater China region, so employers can afford to be choosy – and one of the things they look for in the people they hire today is a good working level of English. English is important.

Yet even though this situation has been apparent for years, and even as China evolves into a major player in world finance and politics, a great many Chinese – including many of those same university graduates – cannot meet the challenge set forth by the Polytechnic University study: they lack the good written English that today's world demands.

This handbook, *You Can Write Better English*, is designed to correct that shortcoming. The book is not a complete survey of the English language. It will not teach you to speak English: that's a job for the schools. It will not teach you to write *perfect* English: that comes only with practice. The book can, however, help you to improve your written English significantly. It contains lists of rules for writing the English language properly, with clear illustrations of how those rules should be applied.

The rules listed here are valid for anyone. *But this book places special emphasis on the mistakes that native Chinese speakers routinely make when writing in English.*

During more than three decades in Asia, I have come to realize that native Chinese speakers tend to make certain specific mistakes – the same mistakes – in English. I've seen it in the writing of the Hong Kong and mainland students I've taught at The University of Hong Kong. I've seen it in English-language newspaper stories written by Chinese reporters. I've seen it on public signs, on restaurant menus, and in the pronouncements of Chinese businessmen, civil servants and government officials.

It doesn't matter if these Chinese are from the mainland, Hong Kong, Taiwan or one of the Southeast Asian nations; identical mistakes crop up in their written English over and over again.

It could be as simple a mistake as leaving the word "the" out of a sentence. That might seem a small matter, but as the rules of good writing listed below note, leaving out or changing a single word in a sentence can lead to misunderstanding, and misunderstanding – in business communications, especially – can lead to disaster. People act on what they read; with the speed of today's communications, they often act within minutes. A sentence sent from one part of the world at 9 a.m. can lead to millions of dollars being spent in other parts of the world by 9:15 a.m. If that sentence contains inaccurate or misleading information, it can cost a lot of people a lot of money.

In the world of business, therefore, clear and accurate writing is essential. But the rules apply whether you're writing a business letter, a public notice, a financial analysis, a memo for your colleagues, a press release, or a newspaper story. In today's globalized world, good written English is something that all professionals should aspire to.

Studying and applying the rules in this handbook can help you toward that goal. Making the small but important corrections listed here can result in a dramatic improvement in your written English.

* * *

But be aware: there are complications to any discussion of "correct" English.

The first complication is the differences between British and American English. English was spread as a global language by two different nations during two different time periods: Great Britain during its years of empire, from the 17th to the mid-20th centuries; and America since the end of World War Two.

Although citizens of Britain and America normally understand each other with no difficulty, British and American English contain many differences, and these differences sometimes affect the rules of writing. Some of the rules of punctuation (the use of periods, commas, quotation marks and other grammatical marks) differ from American to British English. Some objects have different names depending on who is naming them: what the British call a car's "bonnet," Americans call a "hood;" what the Brits call the "hood," Americans call the "top." Some words are pronounced exactly the same, but spelled differently: the British write "*programme*," for example, while the Americans write "*program*." Which one is the "correct" spelling?

There is no simple answer to that question. A rule of English that is valid in Hong Kong, which was a British colony for 156 years, might not be valid in other countries of East Asia, where English has been influenced more by the United States. *The South China Morning Post*, Hong Kong's largest English-language newspaper, uses British English, while just across the border, *China Daily*, China's state-owned English-language newspaper, employs American spellings and usage.

Even within Hong Kong itself, there is a clash between the two styles of English. Due to the territory's British heritage, British spelling and usage are taught in most local schools. But Hong Kong, like much of the world, has been strongly influenced by American culture – movies, television shows, pop songs, Internet terminology – and American spellings and American rules of speech have also crept into everyday use as a result.

Therefore, it is not always possible to say that this or that rule for written English is the correct one. Individuals and organizations at any rate should be aware of the differences between the two styles, choose one or the other, and use it consistently.

Differences between "British" and "American" are noted throughout this book where they are applicable. As a further aid, a comparison of British and American spellings and usage is found in Section 2. (The book itself is written in American English.)

Fortunately, most of the mistakes that native Chinese speakers routinely make in English do not involve these conflicting rules. Therefore, it is fairly easy to point out what the common mistakes are, and to show, without confusion, how they can be corrected.

* * *

A second complicating factor in determining "correct" English is the many exceptions to the rules. While it is easy to state a rule, there is almost always a case in which the rule can legitimately be broken. English, as the little ditty quoted in Section 3 states, is "a crazy language."

Therefore, be warned: terms like "in general," "usually," and "in most cases," will appear throughout this book. These terms are a reminder: the rules are not followed in all cases. If you want to write good English, you will have to learn the exceptions along with the rules.

Barry Kalb
Hong Kong
2010

TABLE OF CONTENTS

CHAPTER ONE
Some Rules of Good Writing

Let's start with a list of rules to keep in mind when writing in English.

There are many lists like this. Some are aimed at anyone who might write occasionally; others are aimed at people who write for a living; still others are aimed specifically at people for whom English is a second language.

Because they are written for different groups, the contents of these lists will often vary. There are certain rules for writing good English, however, that apply to everyone:

1. **Keep it simple**. Don't add unnecessary words or phrases to a sentence. Use the fewest words necessary to make your point. Longer is *not* better.

2. **Get to the point**. Decide what you want to say, and then say it, right at the start. Don't make your readers wait five, seven, ten paragraphs before you tell them what it's all about.

3. **Make it understandable.** You must write clearly. You must explain situations and sequences of events simply and in words the average reader can understand. If nobody can understand what you've written, you have wasted everybody's time.

4. **Every single word you write is important**. Changing one word can change the entire meaning of a sentence. A careless choice of words can lead to misunderstanding. Think about what you're writing, look it over after you've written it, and make sure you really said what you meant to say.

* *Several good habits will help make your writing easier to understand:*

5. **Always keep your audience in mind**. Ask yourself who will likely be reading what you write, or whom you are aiming at, and use information and references that will be understandable to those people. If you're writing about China for an audience in the United States, for example, don't refer to obscure names and events that Americans are unlikely to know about. Similarly...

6. **Explain as you go along. Do *not* assume that your reader knows what you are writing about**. If you refer to something in your writing – an event, an organization, a person – be sure to explain who or what that thing is.

   Anyone moderately familiar with modern history will know that "*The Great Depression*" refers to a period of severe recession that affected the whole world and lasted for more than ten years prior to World War II, and normally no explanation is needed for the term. But many young people do not know about "*The Crash of 1987*," a frightening but very brief global stock market crash that occurred in 1987.

   A brief explanatory phrase should follow the reference, to help the reader understand: "*The Crash of 1987: the day in October of that year when stock markets across the world fell dramatically*."

   If you are writing for an audience of Chinese historians or economists, it's okay to refer to the 1978 "Reform and Opening" without further explanations. But for a general audience, you have to explain what the term means: "Deng Xiaoping's 1978 policy of 'Reform and Opening,' which exposed the Chinese economy to the outside world, and set the stage for today's rapid economic growth."

7. **Organize your facts in logical order**. When you're writing about a topic, complete the information about that topic *before* you go on to the next one. Don't jump randomly from one topic to another. If you're describing a sequence of events, it's usually best to list the events in the order in which they actually occurred.

8. **Deal with only one topic per paragraph**. If you're going to introduce a new topic, do it in a new paragraph.

9. **When switching from one topic to another, it often helps to write a transitional sentence or phrase**. If you suddenly start writing about a new topic, even if you follow Rule 8 above, there's a risk your readers will be confused. A sentence or phrase introducing the new topic can help the reader to follow along.

   Here are two paragraphs from a story that that appeared in a Hong Kong newspaper:

Two new deaths from the H5N1 bird flu virus were reported today in Indonesia.

The government today announced a new law making it illegal to keep poultry in private homes.

The way this was written will lead a reader to make two incorrect assumptions. First, it appears – incorrectly – that the second event was caused by the first. Second, it appears – also incorrectly – that the new law mentioned in the second paragraph was announced by the Indonesian government.

While both paragraphs do deal with the same general topic – bird flu – the two events in this case were not connected; they just happened to occur on the same day. And the "government" referred to in this Hong Kong newspaper story was the Hong Kong government, not the Indonesian government: the second event took place in Hong Kong.

A simple transitional phrase at the start of the second paragraph (along with the insertion of the words "Hong Kong") would clarify how the two sentences are related, and avoid any misunderstanding:

Two new deaths from the H5N1 bird flu virus were reported today in Indonesia.

***In an attempt to prevent the spread of the virus here**, the **Hong Kong** government today announced a new law making it illegal to keep poultry in private homes.*

10. **Quote only one person in a paragraph**. If you quote more than one person in a paragraph, it makes it difficult for the reader to figure out who is speaking.

* *Certain things should be avoided when writing:*

11. **Avoid repetition**. If you've said something once, that's usually enough. Don't use the same word or phrase over and over. Don't repeat full names and titles over and over. Identify the head of the Chinese government as "President Hu Jintao" the first time you refer to him, and only the first time. Your readers will get it. If you mention him again, use a shortened form of his name: "Mr. Hu," or "President Hu," or just "Hu." (*See Rule 23 about "honorifics" below.*)

12. **Avoid redundancy**. When we say two things are "redundant," we mean that they both perform the same function. For safety reasons, an airliner has a primary steering system and a back-up steering system. The two steering systems perform the same function; they are redundant. It's the same with two words or phrases that convey the same idea: they are redundant. Back-up systems are important on airliners, but redundancies make for bad writing.

EXAMPLE: The initials "*a.m.*" and "*in the morning*" mean the same thing. The phrase "*4 a.m. in the morning*," which is the way many people write, is redundant and therefore bad writing. Make your choice: "*4 a.m.*" or "four in the morning."

EXAMPLE: "*The crash scene was littered with dead bodies.*" The phrase "*dead bodies*" is a redundancy. The "bodies" in this case are automatically "dead:" if they were alive, they wouldn't be "bodies," they would be "people." "*The crash scene was littered with bodies*" is much better.

13. **Don't state the obvious**. Don't waste your readers' time by telling them what they already know. If you are writing about a major crime, and the police are on the scene, you don't have to tell your readers that "*the police are investigating the case.*" Of course they're investigating the case: that's their job. The matter would only be worth mentioning if they were *not* investigating the case – which would be highly unusual, and worthy of note.

14. **Avoid jargon and "babble."** "*Jargon*" refers to words and phrases that are used by a particular group or organization, and which are not necessarily understood by outsiders. There is, for example, medical jargon, legal jargon, technical jargon. Avoid this kind of "insider" wording when you write. Use words and phrases the average person reading your work is likely to understand. If you're writing about a new computer technology, for example, and your audience is the general public, don't use complex technical terms that only computer specialists can understand.

"*Babble*" refers to unnecessary, fancy-sounding words that really don't mean much of anything to anybody. Don't throw a lot of fancy words into a sentence just to try to impress your reader with how many words you know. You will only succeed in driving the reader away.

15. **Avoid initials enclosed in parentheses**. Some people automatically add initials in parentheses (or "brackets," as the British call them) any time they refer to an organization or branch of an organization: "the World Health Organization (WHO);" "the Hong Kong Government Social Welfare Department (HKGSWD);" "The University of Hong Kong (HKU)." This is bad writing. It slows the reader down. It makes your text look like a scientific treatise or a mathematical formula. It violates the first rule of good writing: Keep it simple.

Adding initials after the name is useful only in this situation: if you plan to refer to the organization repeatedly in your text, a few short initials are better than spelling out the entire, long name over and over again (*see Rule 11 above about avoiding repetition*). In that case, it helps to add the initials after the *first time* you use the full name, so the reader has no doubt what the initials stand for when they show up later in the text. But if you don't plan to use the initials again, leave them out altogether.

Also, there's no need to add the initials after the name if it is already obvious to your readers what the initials stand for. If you are writing about The University of Hong Kong, and you are writing on a University of Hong Kong website, it's not necessary to write, "*The University of Hong Kong (HKU).*" If "HKU" appears later in your copy, your readers will know what the initials stand for. Remember Rule 5: Always keep your audience in mind.

16. **Avoid exclamation marks, except in direct quotations**. Exclamation marks are common in Chinese-language texts. In English, they make you, the writer, look immature.

17. **Avoid starting a sentence with a dependent clause**. "*Born in Shanghai, Huang became a university professor at the age of 28.*" In sentences like this, the first clause often has no relation to the second – where Mr. Huang was born had nothing to do with his becoming a professor – and using this form often introduces serious grammatical mistakes.

Instead, break the sentence into two straightforward sentences. "*Huang was born in Shanghai. He became a university professor at the age of 28.*"

19. **Not every noun requires an adjective. Not every verb requires an adverb**. Use adjectives and adverbs sparingly, and only when they are necessary to make a point. Don't be afraid to let a noun or a verb stand alone.

20. **Avoid hyperbole: not every adjective or adverb has to be a superlative**. Not everything is "the best," "leading," "cutting-edge," "state-of-the-art," "ground-breaking." Some things are just good, or adequate. Don't feel that you have to tell your reader how wonderful everything and everybody is. Don't automatically write that a speech was "memorable" or "scintillating" or "unforgettable" (many speeches are quite boring). Not everyone who speaks at an event is "honored" or "revered." Don't write that someone thanked his audience "sincerely" (maybe he was actually being *in*sincere). It's bad writing, and it looks like you, the writer, are being insincere. Leave the superlatives and value judgments out of your writing, and just tell people what happened. It makes for much more efficient communication.

21. **Avoid the temptation to describe a person's tone of voice or facial expression each time you use a quote**: "I am going to graduate with honors," *he said with determination*; "I'm afraid I didn't study hard enough for the exam," *she frowned*.

    Sometimes, this kind of description is necessary, but adding it every time is bad writing – and the second example is bad English: a person cannot "frown" a sentence. Ninety-nine percent of the time, a simple *"he said"* or *"she said"* is the best way to attribute a quotation.

22. **Avoid qualifiers**. Words that express judgment (or lack of conviction) on your part should be used sparingly: "He *certainly* succeeded in doing a good job on the assignment;" "The audience was *very* delighted with the performance;" "The workers were *so* happy that the project was finally finished;" "They got the job done *pretty* quickly;" "We all have to try a *little* harder." Each of these sentences is perfectly adequate without the qualifier.

* *Some additional rules that will help your writing:*

23. **When you use quotations, make sure the reader can figure out who is talking**. As noted in Rule 10, if you quote two people in the same

paragraph, it can be difficult for a reader to figure out who is saying what.

Also, if a quote includes several sentences in a row from the *same* person, place the attribution after the first sentence, so the reader doesn't have to wait until the end of the last sentence to learn who is talking. Here's an example from a story about several Hong Kong journalists who were detained by the police while covering a demonstration. In the original version, the attribution doesn't appear until after the fourth and final sentence:

BAD: "We didn't make gestures that incited the demonstrators. We did everything by the book. I never thought that they would say we were causing trouble. I'm deeply disappointed," *said Lam Chun Wai, a TV cameraman who was detained.*

Here's the way it should be written, with the attribution after the first sentence:

GOOD: "We didn't make gestures that incited the demonstrators," *said Lam Chun Wai, a TV cameraman who was and detained.* "We did everything by the book. I never thought that they would say we were causing trouble. I'm deeply disappointed."

Also, don't end a paragraph with a quote by one person, and then immediately start the next paragraph with a quote by a second person; the reader will think the person in the first paragraph is still talking. Look at these two paragraphs:

BAD: "We feel very strongly that this legislation is in the best interests of the public," *the government spokesman said.* "We are confident that the bill will be passed quickly by the legislature."

"I think it's going to take a long time for this bill to be voted on, and I'll be quite surprised if it passes at all in its current form. We think the proposed law would be bad for the economy," *a member of the opposition party said.*

In this example, until the reader reaches the second attribution ("*a member of the opposition party said*"), it looks like the government spokesman is still speaking – and not only that, it looks like he's contradicting what he said in the previous paragraph. A transitional phrase introducing the new speaker is needed between the two paragraphs to avoid confusion.

GOOD: "We feel very strongly that this legislation is in the best interests of the public," *the government spokesman said*. "We are confident that the bill will be passed quickly by the legislature."

A member of the opposition party, however, was skeptical about the bill's chances for passage. "I think it's going to take a long time for this bill to be voted on, and I'll be quite surprised if it passes at all in its current form," *the party member said*. "We think the proposed law would be bad for the economy."

24. **Adopt and use a consistent style on honorifics and courtesy titles**. These are words like *Mr., Ms., Professor, Doctor*. The first time you refer to a person, spell out the person's *full* name and *full* title. After that "first reference," some organizations use honorifics, while others don't use them at all.

EXAMPLES: In the first reference, it is "*Chinese Premier Wen Jiabao*" – full name, full title. In subsequent references ("the second reference"), it should be "*Premier Wen*" or "*Mr. Wen*" (with the honorific), or just "*Wen*" (with no honorific), depending on your organization's style.

In the first reference, "*Bill Gates, the founder of Microsoft*;" in subsequent references, "*Mr. Gates*," or just "*Gates*," again depending on the style of whomever you are writing for.

Whichever style is chosen, make sure you use it consistently throughout your writing. Don't write "*Mr. Gates*" in one sentence and "*Gates*" in the next.

NOTE: American English calls for a period (or full stop) after all abbreviated honorifics (like Mr. or Dr.), while British English omits the full stop in most cases. It would be "*Mr.* Gates" in American, but "*Mr* Gates" in British, for example. (*See a fuller discussion in the "Punctuation" section of Chapter 3*).

26. **Be selective**.   Whatever you write does not have to include every available fact. Pick only the facts, figures and quotes that are necessary to make your writing complete and understandable. Remember Rule 1: Keep it simple.

* One final, extremely important rule:

27.   **Edit yourself**. This is probably the rule that can help you more than any other to improve your writing.   Unfortunately, it's a rule that writers frequently ignore.   After you have finished writing, but *before* you send your work out, read it over again.   If you have the time, take a lengthy break between writing and re-reading, to clear your mind.   Then look for mistakes, omissions, unnecessary words and bad writing, and correct them.

Then read it over a second time.   And a third, if you have time.   You will be amazed at how much better a piece of writing can become if you look it over several times with a careful eye.

CHAPTER TWO
A few words about "American" vs. "British"

People writing about the English language like to quote the Irish playwright George Bernard Shaw, whose life spanned the 19th and 20th centuries.

"Great Britain and America," Shaw wrote, "are nations separated by a common language."

In the 21st century, with the speed of modern communications, the differences between "British" and "American" are growing smaller, and "American" seems to be winning the day. It is now common, for example, to hear broadcasters on the BBC, once a bastion of correct British English, use the American term "a *billion* dollars" instead of the more traditional (and more British) "a *thousand million* dollars." British editors have also been adopting such Americanisms as the suffix *–ize*, with a "*z*," instead of the traditional British *–ise*, with an "*s*."

Nevertheless, quite a few differences still exist. This is especially apparent in the former British colony of Hong Kong. Institutions including the government, the courts, The University of Hong Kong, the public school system and others tend to use British English. But Hong Kong's cinemas and television are filled with American-made movies and drama series, which of course use American English. As a result, terms such as "lift" and "elevator," "flat" and "apartment," have become virtually interchangeable in Hong Kong's daily English conversation.

It is therefore impossible to say one or the other is "correct," and for someone trying to learn English, this can be confusing. This is especially true when it comes to writing, because some words that are pronounced the same in British and American are spelled differently, so a person has to learn the correct spelling in addition to the correct word.

A person or an organization should choose one style of English or the other, British or American, to use on a regular basis. Whichever you choose, however, you should be aware of the alternative forms of certain words. Here are some of the more common differences:

Names of Objects

British	American
British	**American**
Aluminium	Aluminum
Aubergine	Eggplant
Car park	Parking lot
Courgette	Zucchini
Current account	Checking account
Estate agent	Real estate agent, realtor
Flat	Apartment
Flyover	Overpass
Lift	Elevator
Lorry	Truck
Maize	Corn
Nappy	Diaper
Pavement	Sidewalk
Roundabout	Traffic circle
Subway	Underground passage, underpass
Trainers	Sneakers, running shoes
Underground	Subway, metro
Windscreen	Windshield

In British, the letter "Z" is called a "*Zed*." In American, it is called a "*Zee*."

The British call the little round punctuation mark that typically comes at the end of a sentence (.) a "*full stop*." Americans call it a "*period*." (In computer-related language, both refer to the mark as a "*dot*.")

The British call the half-round symbols placed around a phrase (*like this*) "*brackets*." Americans call them "*parentheses*."

The British call the symbols placed around a quotation (" ") "*inverted commas*." Americans call them "*quotation marks*."

Spelling of Objects

The British and American forms of some words are pronounced the same and mean the same thing, but are spelled differently:

British	American
Cheque	Check
Gaol	Jail
Jewellery	Jewelry
Judgement	Judgment
Kerb	Curb
Programme*	Program
Storey (architecture)	Story
Traveller	Traveler
Tyre	Tire

NOTE: Some British writing guides specify "*program*" when the reference is to a "computer program" (a term popularized in America), but "*programme*" in all other cases.

Other Spelling Differences

The British tend to use the form *–ise* at the end of certain words, where Americans use *–ize*:

British	American
Capitalise	Capitalize
Organise	Organize
Recognise	Recognize
Realise	Realize

The British tend to use *–re* at the end of certain words where Americans use *–er*:

British	American
Centre	Center
Calibre	Caliber
Spectre	Specter

The British tend to use –*our* at the end of certain words where Americans use –*or*:

British	**American**
Colour	Color
Flavour	Flavor
Honour	Honor
Labour	Labor

But:

Glamour	Glamour

NOTE: A proper name should use the official spelling, whether one is writing in British or American. The American holiday is called "Labor Day." The British political party is the "Labour Party."

Additional spelling differences: The British –*ence* often becomes –*ense* ("def*ence*," "def*ense*") in American.

The British add an "*a*" or an "*o*" before the "*e*" in certain words, where Americans do not ("***ae***sthetics," "**e**sthetics;" "**fo**etus," "**fe**tus").

CHAPTER THREE
Grammar: The biggest problem

Learning any new language is a challenge. Memorizing new words – the "vocabulary" – is a lengthy and difficult process, and so is learning correct "syntax," which refers to the way words are strung together in a sentence.

However, "grammar" is what native Chinese speakers wrestle with most frequently when writing (and speaking) English, and *they tend to have special trouble with several particular areas* of grammar. These areas include (A) the group of words known as "articles," (B) singular and plural nouns, and (C) verb tenses. Problems with these areas pop up repeatedly throughout Chinese-speaking societies, whether the words are written by primary school students or business executives or high-ranking government officials.

Simply correcting these grammatical problems can go a long way toward improving your written English. These and other troublesome grammatical points are discussed in detail in this section.

* * *

A: ARTICLES

The words "the," "a" and "an" are known as "*articles.*" There is no exact equivalent of these words in Chinese. In an English-language sentence, articles precede *nouns* or *adjectives*, and the proper use of articles is essential for good written English.

> **NOUNS** are *people* or *things*: "The *woman.*" "A *man.*" "An *automobile.*" Nouns are also *concepts* – things that can be described, but cannot be held in your hand: "The *rule.*" "A *dispute.*" "An *idea.*"

> **ADJECTIVES** are *words that describe nouns.* An adjective can be a color, a number, a measure of size, the place a person lives – any number of things. These are all examples of nouns with adjectives in front of them: "*Green* apples," "*Three* bottles of beer," "*Tall* people," "*Beijing* residents."

Nouns usually require either an article or an adjective in front of them, and sometimes both. It is not correct to write, "Company sent invoice." The correct form is, "*The* company sent *an* invoice." It is not correct to write, "Hong Kong government has passed new banking law." The correct form is, "*The* Hong Kong government has passed *a* new banking law."

> **NO ARTICLE REQUIRED:** "They are *Beijing* residents;" "Americans are *tall* people;" "We drank *three* bottles of beer;" "*Tonight's* meeting will be held early."

> **ARTICLE REQUIRED:** "A survey was taken among *the foreign* residents of Beijing;" "He is a *tall* person," "We drank *the three* bottles of beer that we found in the refrigerator;" "I have to go to *an early* meeting tonight."

One of the most common writing errors made by native Chinese speakers is to leave out the word "the," or to use it where it does not belong. Another common error is to confuse the use of "the" and "a."

> **EXAMPLE:** Here are two of the "main functions" of the Chinese central government's Hong Kong and Macao Affairs Office, as listed on the office's official website. The article "*the*" is misused in both items (*there are also other errors here, which are identified in Chapter Six*):

3. "Be responsible for the working contacts with the Chief Executives of *HKSAR and MCSAR* as well as the governments of the two SARs."

4. "Promote and coordinate *the cooperation* and exchange in the field of economics, science, technology, education, culture, etc. between the mainland and the two SARs of Hong Kong and Macao."

CORRECT: In number 3, the word "*the*" should appear before both "*HKSAR*" and "*MCSAR*." In number 4, "*the*" should *not* appear before "*cooperation*."

* * *

" A " and " An "

* "*A*" and "*an* " are the equivalent of "one," and they precede only singular nouns.

"*A* man" = "*one* man."

"*An* orange" = "*one* orange."

* "*A*" and "*an*" are general references. They do not refer to a specific person or thing. In general, use "*a*" or "*an*" when it is not clear which person or thing is being referred to.

EXAMPLE: "*A* Hong Kong financial company was accused yesterday of cheating its clients." (In this first reference, we do not know the specific name of the company, so the general article "*a*" is used. On second reference, use "*the* company.")

EXAMPLE: "*An* ethnic Chinese person who is *a* United States citizen is known as *a* 'Chinese-American.'" (No specific Chinese person or U.S. citizen is being referred to, so the general "*an*" and "*a*" are used in all three instances.)

* "*A*" and "*an*" have the same meaning. Which one to use depends on whether the word that follows starts with a consonant or a vowel.

CONSONANTS are the letters *b, c, d, f, g, h, j, k, l, m, n, p, q, r, s, t, v, w, x, y* and *z.*

VOWELS are the letters *a, e, i, o* and *u.*

* "*A*" usually comes before a word that begins with a consonant or a consonant sound.

> **EXAMPLES:** "*A* banana"
>
> "*A* tall man"

* The vowels "*e*" and "*u*" have a consonant sound when they appear at the start of certain words, and these words therefore also take "*a*."

> **EXAMPLES:** "*A* European city"
>
> "*A* university"

* "*An*" comes before a word beginning with a vowel or a vowel sound.

> **EXAMPLES:** "*An* orange"
>
> "*An* intelligent man"

* "*An*" comes before a word starting with "*h*" when the "*h*" sound is not pronounced, as in "*hour*" or "*honorary*."

> **EXAMPLE:** It takes *an* hour and 45 minutes to travel from Hong Kong to Guangzhou by train. (The "*h*" in "*hour*" is silent, so "*an* hour" is correct.)

> **COMPARE:** We have decided to buy *a* house. (The "*h*" sound in "*house*" is pronounced, so "*a* house" is correct.)

> **NOTE:** Traditionally, the word "*historic*" was preceded by the word "*an*," as in, "This is *an* historic building." In American usage, this has generally been discontinued, and the sentence becomes, "This is *a* historic building." The British still tend to use "*an*" before "*historic*."

* "*An*" can also come before a consonant if *the consonant itself has a vowel sound, and if the consonant is pronounced separately.* The consonants "*n*" and "*f*," for example, both begin with a vowel sound ("*en*," "*eff*"). In "N-B-A" (the initials of the National Basketball Association), or "F-B-I" (the initials of the U.S. Federal Bureau of Investigation), the letters are all pronounced separately, so "*an*" is used, as follows:

EXAMPLE: "The Chinese basketball player Yao Ming plays for *an* NBA team." (The letter "*n*" in "NBA" is pronounced separately, so "*an*" is correct.)

COMPARE: "Harbin is *a* northern Chinese city." (The letter "*n*" in "northern" is not pronounced separately, so "*a*" is correct.)

EXAMPLE: "She played the role of *an* FBI agent in a television drama series." (The letter "*f*" in "FBI" is pronounced separately, so "*an*" is correct.)

COMPARE: "She bought *a* fur coat." (The letter "*f*" in "fur" is not pronounced separately, so "*a*" is correct.)

* * *

"The"

* "*The*" can be used before both singular and plural nouns.

>   **EXAMPLES:**   "*The* house"
>
>   "*The* houses"

* "*The*" can be used before words beginning with either vowels or consonants.

>   **EXAMPLES:**   "*The* dog"
>
>   "*The* elephant"

* "*The*" usually refers to a specific thing or things. In general, use "*the*" when it is clear which person or thing you are referring to.

In general, do not use "*the*" when you are referring to something for the first time; do not use it when it is not clear which specific person or thing you are referring to.

EXAMPLE: "*A* man was hit by a bus in Kowloon yesterday. *The* man was pronounced dead on arrival at hospital."

EXPLANATION: In the first sentence the man is not identified, so the general reference "*a* man" is correct. In the second sentence, we now know which specific man is being referred to – the man *who was hit by a bus*, and who was mentioned in the first sentence. Therefore, "*the* man" is correct in the second sentence.

EXAMPLE: "Three men were injured when their car spun off the road yesterday. *The* man *who was driving* was charged with reckless driving."

EXPLANATION: In the first sentence, none of the three men are identified; the word "men" is preceded by an adjective, and no article is needed. In the second sentence, we are referring to a specific man – the one *who was driving* – so "*the* man" is correct.

* "*The*" is always used when you are referring to a thing that is commonly known – *the* Hong Kong government, *the* sun, *the* Great Wall of China, *the* universe – even if you are referring to it for the first time.

* "*The*" is sometimes part of a proper name, in which case it is capitalized:

> **EXAMPLES:** "*The* University of Hong Kong"
>
> "*The* South China Morning Post"

* * *

PRACTICE SENTENCES #1: Insert the correct articles in the following sentences (*answers to all practice sentences can be found in the appendix at the end of this booklet*):

1. ___ former prime minister of Great Britain received ___ honorary degree from ___ University of Hong Kong in recognition of ___ work he had done to combat world hunger.

2. ___ horse, ___ elephant and ___ unidentified third animal all escaped from ___ circus last night.

3. ___ off-duty police officer chased and caught __ mugger who had just robbed ___ couple in ___ Kowloon section of Hong Kong last night. ___ mugger was later identified as ___ same man who had robbed ___ elderly woman ___ hour and ___ half earlier on Hong Kong Island.

4. ___ chief executive of ___ Hong Kong government was quoted today in ___ Times of London as saying ___ vote will be held in ___ Legislative Council on ___ question of universal suffrage in Hong Kong "at ___ appropriate time."

5. In ___ United States, ___ FBI agent is ___ federal officer.

###

B: SINGULARS AND PLURALS

Another of the most common mistakes made by native Chinese speakers is to confuse *singular* and *plural nouns*.

> **A SINGULAR NOUN** refers to one of a thing: One *tree*, a *dog*, an *idea*.

> **A PLURAL NOUN** refers to more than one of the same thing: Two *trees*, some *dogs*, 40 *cats*, many *ideas*.

A Chinese person writing in English will frequently use a singular where a plural is called for, and vice versa. This mistake is seen in all types of writing.

* A Chinese restaurant menu will typically offer "Stir-fried sliced chicken with *mushroom* and *bean sprout*." Does this mean the chef is going to put only *one mushroom* and *one bean sprout* in each serving of the dish? A chef who served such a meager dish would probably not have many customers. But because singular nouns are used ("*mushroom*," "*bean sprout*"), the menu says that's all the customer is going to get.

* A sign at a construction site warns passing drivers: "Danger: beware of *heavy vehicle*." Does that mean there is only one heavy vehicle at the site? If a driver sees one heavy vehicle leaving the site, is there no longer a danger from other heavy vehicles? There's usually more than one heavy vehicle at a construction site, and all such vehicles are potentially dangerous, but this sign tells drivers there is only one vehicle to worry about.

In correct English, plural nouns should be used in both of these cases. The menu should offer stir-fried sliced chicken with "*mushrooms* and *bean sprouts*." The construction sign should warn of "heavy *vehicles*."

* In 2008, a press release by the Democratic Party of Hong Kong referred to a mainland government promise to give foreign reporters more freedom when reporting inside China. The press release, as it appeared on the party's website, read in part like this:

  "In January 2007, *a relaxed reporting rules were* published which supposedly *allow* foreign journalists to report more freely on the mainland."

QUESTION: How many rules were published?

If there was only one rule, the sentence should read: "…a relaxed reporting *rule was* published which supposedly *allows*…"

If there was more than one rule, it should read: "…relaxed reporting *rules were* published which supposedly *allow*…"

The article "*a*," remember, precedes only singular nouns. And the verb ("*was*" or "*were*") has to match the number of things in question ("*a* rule *was* published;" "*several* rules *were* published").

* * *

The confusion over singulars and plurals arises because of the differences in the languages. In Chinese, there is no change in the noun itself whether one thing or many things are being referred to. For example, in Chinese a person would, in effect, speak of "one *book*," "two *book*," "20 *book*," "150 *book*."

In English, however, in almost all cases the noun must be written differently when it changes from a singular to a plural. The word "*book*" has to be made into a plural when it refers to more than one: "one *book*," "two *books*," "150 *books*."

If all plurals were formed simply be adding an "*s*" to the end of the noun, as in the example above, the matter would be relatively simple. But as we said in the introduction, there are exceptions to almost every rule in the English language. There's a well-known ditty about how confusing English can be, and the first part of the ditty discusses plural nouns:

We'll begin with a box, and the plural is boxes,
But the plural of ox becomes oxen, not oxes.

One fowl is a goose, but two are called geese,
Yet the plural of moose should never be meese.

You may find a lone mouse or a nest full of mice,
Yet the plural of house is houses, not hice.

If the plural of man is always called men,
Why shouldn't the plural of pan be called pen?

If I speak of my foot and show you my feet,
And I give you a boot, would a pair be called beet?

If one is a tooth and a whole set are teeth,
Why shouldn't the plural of booth be called beeth?

Then one may be that, and three would be those,
Yet hat in the plural would never be hose,
And the plural of cat is cats, not cose.

We speak of a brother and also of brethren,
But though we say mother, we never say methren…

Let's face it - English is a crazy language.

* * *

Despite all that…the general rule for singulars and plurals is perfectly consistent: If you are talking about only one thing, use the singular form of the noun; if you are talking about more than one thing, use the plural form, however it is written. A number is sometimes used before a plural noun ("*two books*") to indicate how many things you are talking about, but *whether or not there is a number*, the plural form must be used.

> **WRONG:** I bought two *book* today.
> **CORRECT:** I bought two *books* today.
> **CORRECT:** I bought some *books* today (*no number used*).

> **WRONG:** Six *child* were on the bus.
> **CORRECT:** Six *children* were on the bus.
> **CORRECT:** Several *children* were on the bus (*no number used*).

* **EXCEPTION:** A small number of nouns *do not change form* in any way from the singular to the plural. "Fish," for example, can mean one fish, or many fish:

> **SINGULAR:** "I caught *a fish* today."
> **PLURAL:** "We caught *a lot of fish* today."

OTHER NOUNS that are the same in the singular and the plural form include "sheep," "deer," "moose," "cannon" and "species."

* Some nouns are *always* plural. They include "scissors" (there is no such thing as "*one scissor*"), "trousers," "pants," "barracks" and "premises" (when "premises" refers to a building).

> ***Unfortunately, there are no universal rules to tell you when the exceptions apply. You have to learn the exceptions word by word.***

* Some nouns, especially if they are concepts (things that cannot be held in the hand), in most cases *cannot* be made into a plural.

> **WRONG:** I have completed the *researches* for my thesis.
> **CORRECT:** I have completed the *research* for my thesis.

> **WRONG:** The teacher gave us a lot of *homeworks* today.
> **CORRECT:** The teacher gave us a lot of *homework* today.

> **WRONG:** There are *many unrests* in the Muslim world today.
> **CORRECT:** There is *much unrest* in the Muslim world today.

* If a noun is used as an adjective – that is, if it is used to describe another noun – *the singular is used*, not the plural.

> **WRONG:** My mother makes delicious *vegetables* dumplings.
> **CORRECT:** My mother makes delicious *vegetable* dumplings.

* In the case of a compound, hyphenated word – a "word" composed of more than one word – usually *the main word only* is made into a plural.

> **WRONG:** All three of my brother-in-*laws* were at the family dinner.
> **CORRECT:** All three of my *brothers-in-law* were at the family dinner.

> **WRONG:** Two passer-*bys* were injured when the terrorist bomb went off.
> **CORRECT:** Two *passers*-by were injured when the terrorist bomb went off.

* However, in the common phrase indicating how old a person or thing is – an "*XX- year-old*" person – *no* word in the phrase should be made into a plural, and the words have to be hyphenated.

> **WRONG:** Native Chinese speakers will often, incorrectly, write this: "The winner of the lottery was a 37 *years* old man (*no hyphens, "years" written in the plural*)."

> **CORRECT:** "The winner of the lottery was a 37-*year*-old man (*hyphens used, "year" written in the singular*)."

* * *

* Most plurals are formed simply by adding an "*s*" after the final letter.

SINGULAR: *Boy*	**PLURAL:** *Boys*
SINGULAR: *Idea*	**PLURAL:** *Ideas*

* In British English, numerals and strings of initials that form a word are also made plural by adding an "*s*."

SINGULAR: *1990*	**PLURAL:** *The 1990s*
SINGULAR: *A 10 and a 20*	**PLURAL:** *10s and 20s*
SINGULAR: *A Boeing 747*	**PLURAL:** *Boeing 747s*
SINGULAR: *An IOU*	**PLURAL:** *IOUs*

* Americans are more likely than the British to add an apostrophe to plural numbers and initials made into words. (*See the section "American" vs. "British" for a more detailed discussion of the differences between the two forms of English.*)

SINGULAR: *1990*	**PLURAL:** *The 1990's*
SINGULAR: *A 10 and a 20*	**PLURAL:** *10's and 20's*
SINGULAR: *An IOU*	**PLURAL:** *IOU's*

* In both British and American English, *individual letters* are made plural by adding both an apostrophe and an "*s*."

> **SINGULAR:** *He received an A in English.*

> **PLURAL:** *Several people in the class received A's in English.* (If the apostrophe were not added, the second sentence would read, "*Several people in the class received **As** in English*," which would be confusing.)

> **PLURAL:** *He dotted his i's and crossed his t's.* (If the apostrophes were not added, this sentence would read, "*He dotted his **is** and crossed his **ts***," which would be confusing.)

* Nouns that end in "*ey*" are usually made plural by adding an "*s*."

SINGULAR: *Monkey*   **PLURAL:** *Monkeys*
SINGULAR: *Turkey*   **PLURAL:** *Turkeys*

* However, nouns that end in "*y*" without the "*e*" are usually made plural by dropping the "*y*" and adding "*ies*."

SINGULAR: *Duty*   **PLURAL:** *Duties*
SINGULAR: *Fairy*   **PLURAL:** *Fairies*

* Nouns that end in "*s*," such as "bus" and "kiss," are usually made plural by adding an "*es*" after the final "*s*."

SINGULAR: *Bus*   **PLURAL:** *Buses*
SINGULAR: *Kiss*   **PLURAL:** *Kisses*

* The same rule applies to names ending with an "*s*."

SINGULAR: Mr. *Jones*
PLURAL (referring to the whole family): the *Joneses*.

* Nouns that end in "*ch*," "*sh*" and "*x*" also are usually made plural by adding an "*es*."

SINGULAR: *Church*   **PLURAL:** *Churches*
SINGULAR: *Ash*   **PLURAL:** *Ashes*
SINGULAR: *Fox*   **PLURAL:** *Foxes*

* Some nouns that end in the letter "*o*" form the plural by adding "*es*."

SINGULAR: Potato   **PLURAL:** Potatoes
SINGULAR: Tomato   **PLURAL:** Tomatoes
SINGULAR: Hero   **PLURAL:** Heroes
SINGULAR: Echo   **PLURAL:** Echoes

* However, some nouns that end with the letter "o" simply take an "*s*."

SINGULAR: Memo   **PLURAL:** Memos
SINGULAR: Zero   **PLURAL:** Zeros
SINGULAR: Auto   **PLURAL:** Autos
SINGULAR: Motto   **PLURAL:** Mottos

* Some words (as the ditty at the beginning of this section illustrates) have a plural that is very different from the singular:

SINGULAR: Person	**PLURAL:** People
SINGULAR: Mouse	**PLURAL:** Mice
SINGULAR: Child	**PLURAL:** Children

* Some words form the plural by changing a single letter in the middle of the word:

SINGULAR: Ma*n*	**PLURAL:** Me*n*
SINGULAR: Bas*i*s	**PLURAL:** Bas*e*s

* Some words change a letter *and* add an "*s*" or "*es*":

SINGULAR: Wi*f*e	**PLURAL:** Wi*ves*
SINGULAR: Hoo*f*	**PLURAL:** Hoo*ves*
BUT: Roof	**PLURAL:** Roofs

Again, there are no universal rules to tell you when the different forms apply, and you will have to learn the exceptions individually.

* * *

ADDITIONAL NOTES:

* Three words that cause native Chinese speakers a lot of trouble are "*audience*," "*staff*" and "*talent*."

1. *Audience* does not refer to an individual person; it is a group of people viewing or listening to an event *at the same time.* There can be two different *audiences* in two different theaters, but all the people in the same theater comprise one single *audience.*

2. An individual person can have many *talents*, but when the word refers to talented people, *talent* is a general concept and does not take a plural.

3. Similarly, *staff* refers to a group of employees working for the same company. There can be several *staffs* at several different companies, but all the employees at the same company comprise one single *staff.*

WRONG: "Most of the *audiences* agreed that last night's performance at the university theater was excellent."

CORRECT: "The *audience* said last night's performance was excellent," or, "Most *members of the audience* agreed that last night's performance was excellent."

WRONG: "We recruited several new talents for the company."

CORRECT: "We recruited new talent for the company."

WRONG: "Five *staffs* resigned from the company today."

CORRECT: "Five *members of the staff* resigned today," or, more simply, "Five *employees* resigned today."

* Another word that causes many native Chinese speakers trouble – a word that looks like a plural but is not – is "*overseas*." Chinese will often write "*oversea*," without the final "*s*," which is incorrect: "*oversea*" is not a word. The final "*s*" has to be there, whether the word is used as an adjective ("*overseas* Chinese") or as a location ("He spent a year *overseas*").

* Some words used by many people today as singulars, such as "*data*" and "*media*," are actually plurals.

It is incorrect to write, "The data *shows* that air pollution is increasing." The correct English is, "The data *show* that air pollution is increasing."

The singular of "*media*" is "*medium*," as in "television is a news *medium*." It is becoming increasingly common for people, including reporters for the BBC, to use "media" as a singular when referring to the news media: "The media *is* exaggerating the impact of the event." Common or not, this is bad English. It should be, "The media *are* exaggerating the impact of the event."

###

C: VERB TENSES

A verb is an action word: it tells what's happening. "I *go,*" "You *study,*" "He (she, it) *says,*" "We *write,*" "They *cooperate.*" The different forms of "*to be*" are also verbs: "I *am,*" "you *are,*" "he (or she or it) *is,*" "we *are,*" "they *are.*"

> **THE INFINITIVE** is the basic form of a verb. It is formed by combining the verb with the word "*to:*" "*to come,*" "*to go,*" "*to be,*" "*to run.*"

A verb's *tense* indicates when the action took place, or is *taking* place, or is *going* to take place, or *might* take place. Verb tenses are another element of English that do not have an exact equivalent in Chinese. They can be doubly difficult because some forms of one verb can be spelled the same as a different form of a second verb (*see the discussion of "find" and "found," "grind" and "ground," at the end of this section*).

The most frequently used verb tenses in English are (A) **PRESENT TENSE**, (B) **PROGRESSIVE TENSE**, (C) **PAST TENSE**, (D) **PRESENT PERFECT TENSE**, (E) **PAST PERFECT TENSE**, (F) **FUTURE TENSE** and (G) **CONDITIONAL TENSE**. Using the wrong tense in a sentence can make it difficult for a reader to understand what is happening, or when the action took place. The wrong verb tense can change the entire meaning of a sentence and can lead to misunderstanding, and in any case it's bad English.

In early 2010, Hong Kong Financial Secretary John Tsang appeared on a radio program to answer the public's questions about the 2010-2011 government budget. Afterward, he answered reporters' questions, and this was one of his answers (which was posted on the Hong Kong government website):

> "We've *push* out a basket of measures already, and we do have other *measure* ready, *in depending on the situation how it evolves.*"

Along with some badly garbled English ("*in depending on the situation how it evolves*") and an incorrect singular noun ("*measure*" *instead of* "*measures*"), Mr. Tsang was guilty of getting his verb tense wrong. He should have said, "We've *pushed* out a basket…" instead of "We've *push* out a basket…" One of the highest-ranking government officials in Hong Kong should speak better English than this.

Native Chinese speakers tend to have particular trouble with the correct use of the **PAST PERFECT TENSE** *("I had gone"), and they almost invariably confuse the use of "will" and "would."*

* * *

A. The **PRESENT TENSE** indicates an action that *has not yet been completed* or is *ongoing*, or an action that *is habitual*.

> "I *see* the man."
> "You *work* in an advertising agency."
> "He (she, it) *moves* very fast."
> "We *attend* a lecture on accounting every Monday."
> "They *go* to the same restaurant every week."

B. The **PROGRESSIVE TENSE** is formed by adding "*-ing*" to the end of a verb ("sing" + "ing" = "singing"). This new word is combined with a form of the verb "*to be*."

> "I *am singing* my favorite song."
> "You *are working* very hard today."
> "He [or she or it] is *waiting* for the minibus to arrive."
> "We *are eating* our lunch."
> "They *are playing* basketball."

The **PROGRESSIVE TENSE** is used:

1. To describe something that *is happening* at this moment, or *will be happening* at a specific time in the future:

> "I *am reading* that newspaper right now. You can read it after I've finished."
> "She *is washing* the dishes."
> "The neighbors *are making* an awful lot of noise."
> "I *am flying* to Beijing early tomorrow morning."

2. To describe an action that is ongoing:

> "I *am attending* a university in the United States."
> "I find that I *am worrying* a lot about my health lately."
> "I *am crossing* the border for business on a regular basis these days."

C. The **PAST TENSE** is used when the action *has been completed*, sometimes (but not always) at *a specific time* in the past.

> "I *saw* the doctor *on March 17th* (*specific time mentioned*)."
> "They *made* a lot of noise *last night* (*specific time mentioned*)."
> "He doesn't live here any longer. He *moved* to a new flat (*no specific time mentioned*)."

D. The **PRESENT PERFECT TENSE** is formed by combining the **PRESENT TENSE** of the verb "to have" with the **PAST PARTICIPLE** of another verb:

> **PRESENT TENSE**: I "*go*."
> **PRESENT PERFECT TENSE**: I "*have gone*."

The **PRESENT PERFECT TENSE** is used:

1. When something happened at *an indefinite time* in the past: "I *have seen* that movie twice (*no specific time mentioned*)."

   COMPARE this with use of the **PAST TENSE**: "I *saw* that movie twice last month (*action completed at a specific time*)."

2. When something *is still happening*, or *might be happening again* in the future: "Every item in the department store *has been* on sale since the beginning of the month (*event still happening*)."

   "The South China Morning Post *has published* articles on the democracy debate in Hong Kong (*and is likely to publish further articles*)."

   "He *has been* in trouble with the police before (*and might be in trouble again*)."

E. The **PAST PERFECT TENSE** is formed by combining the **PAST TENSE** of the verb "to have" with the **PAST PARTICIPLE** of another verb.

> **PRESENT TENSE**: I "*go*."
> **PAST PERFECT TENSE**: I "*had gone*."

The **PAST PERFECT TENSE** is used when an action you are describing (**ACTION #1**) took place before a second action (**ACTION #2**).

"Luckily, *I* **had read** *that chapter* (**ACTION #1, PAST PERFECT TENSE**) before *I* **took** *the exam* (**ACTION #2**) yesterday."

"He **had eaten** *Chinese food* (**ACTION #1, PAST PERFECT TENSE**) only once before *he* **visited** *Hong Kong* (**ACTION #2**)."

The **PAST PERFECT TENSE** may *not* be used as a *substitute* for the **PAST TENSE** or the **PRESENT PERFECT TENSE**:

WRONG: I *had eaten* my breakfast at 6 o'clock this morning.

CORRECT: I *ate* my breakfast at 6 o'clock this morning (*action completed at a specific time; use the* **PAST TENSE**).

CORRECT: I *have eaten* my breakfast (*no specific time mentioned; use the* **PRESENT PERFECT TENSE**).

* * *

There are two tenses that native Chinese speakers almost invariably confuse when writing in English: the **FUTURE TENSE** and the **CONDITIONAL TENSE**. *One of the most common of all writing errors is to use "would" when the correct word is "will."*

F.   The **FUTURE TENSE** is formed by combining a verb with the word "*will.*"

"I *will be* at the office by 9 o'clock."
"I *will take* the afternoon flight to Beijing."

The **FUTURE TENSE** is used to denote *future action that is certain*:

"The Chef Executive *will* visit Beijing next week."

G.   The **CONDITIONAL TENSE** is formed by combining a verb with the words "*would*," "*could*" or "*should*."

"I *would* go."
"I *should* stay."
"I *could* join you."

The **CONDITIONAL TENSE** generally indicates that an action is *possible, but not certain*: it *is possible* that such-and-such a thing *might happen*, but only *on the condition* that something else does or does not happen. Or, it indicates that a particular thing *will not happen* because of some other action.

USE THE CONDITIONAL TENSE:

1. when it is *not certain* that an action will take place: "I *would* go to the Rugby 7s...*if I could* find a ticket."

   COMPARE this with use of the **FUTURE TENSE**, indicating an action that *is certain*: "I *will* be going to the Rugby 7s...*because my brother bought a ticket for me.*"

2. when a desired event cannot take place because of some other factor:

   "I *would* be delighted to join you for dinner tomorrow...*but I can't, because I have to work late.*"

   I *should* go to my university class tomorrow...*but I have to take my sick mother to the doctor.*"

   "I *could* finish the project this evening...*but then I would miss the office party.*"

3. to indicate habitual or repeated action in the past:

   "When he was young, he *would* get up early every morning to study before he went to school."

   Remember: The word "would" is NOT a substitute for the word "will."

   NOTE: In formal English, the **FUTURE TENSE** under certain conditions calls for "*shall*" instead of "*will*" ("I *shall* be there on time"), and the **CONDITIONAL TENSE** calls for "*should*" instead of "*would*" ("We should be delighted to join you for dinner tomorrow").

However, like many other elements of speech, these two have largely fallen out of use in modern-day English. It is common today – and perfectly acceptable in most situations – to say, "I *will* be there on time," "We *would* be delighted to join you..."

The most common uses of "*shall*" today are in such questions as "Shall we go?" or "Shall we dance?" or such historic phrases as "We shall overcome!"

* * *

The most common way to form the **PAST TENSE** of a verb is to add *–ed* to the end of the verb ("He *calculated* the number," "She *waxed* the floor," "He *hammered* the nail"). But as with singulars and plurals, there are numerous exceptions: there are many other ways this tense is formed. The past tense of "make," for example, is "made." The past tense of "understand" is "understood."

Even when all the forms of verbs are memorized – and there are many of them to memorize – there are some special dangers lurking in the language. Here are several examples:

"Find" and "Found"

The verb "to *find*," meaning to locate something, is a common enough word, and even people who speak only moderately good English usually know that the **PAST TENSE** of the verb is "*found*." What a lot of non-native English speakers don't realize is that "to *found*" is also an entirely separate verb, which means "*to establish, to set up*." In this case, the **PAST TENSE** is "*founded*." An item that is lost can be "*found*." A company or an organization can be "*founded*." Examples:

1. **PRESENT TENSE:**   I'm trying to *find* my keys.
   PAST TENSE: I *found* my keys.
2. **PRESENT TENSE:**   It was only in the last two years that they were able put together enough start-up capital to *found* the company.
   PAST TENSE: The company was *founded* two years ago.

* * *

"Grind" and "Ground"

Similarly, the past tense of the verb "to *grind*," meaning to chop something into small bits with the help of a machine, is *"ground."* But "to *ground"* is also an entirely separate verb, which means to restrict the movement of a vessel (an airplane or a ship) or, in informal language, a person. In this case, the past tense is "grounded." Meat or flour can be *"ground."* An airplane, a ship or a person can be *"grounded."* Examples:

1. **PRESENT TENSE:** I'm getting ready to *grind* the beef for tonight's dinner.

   PAST TENSE: We *ground* the beef for the hamburgers yesterday.

   ADJECTIVE FORM: I bought some *ground* beef from the butcher.

2. **PRESENT TENSE:** If the weather gets any worse, we're going to have to *ground* all flights.

   PAST TENSE: We have *grounded* all flights due to bad weather.

3. **INFORMAL USAGE:** *A parent says to a teenage child*: "If you don't do your homework, I'm going to *ground* you for the weekend." (I'm not going to let you go out with your friends.) *The child tells his friend*: "I can't go out with you tonight. I've been *grounded*."

* * *

"Lie" and "Lay"

Native and non-native English speakers both tend to confuse these two verbs. "To lie" is something you do to yourself: "I'm tired. I'm going to *lie* down for awhile." (*"To lie" also means to tell a falsehood*.) "To lay" is something you do to another object: "This backpack is getting very heavy. I'm going to *lay* it down for awhile;" "The purpose of this meeting is to *lay* out the terms of the deal."

These two verbs cause plenty of confusion in the **PRESENT TENSE**. Additional problems come with the **PAST TENSES** and **PAST PARTICPLES** of the verbs.

* The **PAST TENSE** of "lie' is "lay:" "He was tired, so he *lay* down for awhile."

* The **PAST PARTICIPLE** of "lie" is "lain:" "He *had* only *lain* down for a short time before his alarm clock rang."

* The **PAST TENSE** of "lay" is "laid:" "He *laid* out all the terms of the deal;" "Several people in my company were *laid* off today because of the bad economy."

* The **PAST PARTICPLE** of "lay" is also "laid:" "He's been working for six straight hours and he *hasn't laid* his tools down yet."

* * *

Practice Sentences #2: Fill in the correct forms and tenses of the verbs in parentheses. (Some sentences can have more than one correct answer, depending on the time period that is being depicted.)

1. The weather (*to be*) terrible these last few days. It (*to be*) raining so hard our dog (*not to go*) outside for his regular walk.

2. I (*to study*) nonstop for the past five days. I think I (*to be*) ready for the final exam.

3. If you (*to take*) more time, you (*not to forget*) to pack your presentation materials.

4. I (*to move*) into this flat just last April, and now I (*to move*) again.

5. My friend (*to have*) a very dangerous job. Every time I (*to see*) him, I'm afraid it (*to be*) the last.

6. I (*to go*) to China every week for business. I almost feel as if I (*to live*) there.

7. I (*to see*) the movie twice already, and I (*to see*) it again this evening.

8. He (*to lie*) down for only a few minutes before the alarm rang and he had (*to get*) up again.

9. I (*to compete*) in a dozen marathons before I (*to enter*) the big New York Marathon last year.

10. He (*to lay*) down the sack of cement and then (*to lie*) down to take a short nap.

11. It took us six hours of tramping around the fields, but we finally (*to lay*) out the boundaries of the property. I got so tired at one point that I (*to lie*) down on a rock to rest. We plan to (*to lay*) out the boundary of the second plot tomorrow.

12. We were ordered (*to grind*) the flour from 8 a.m. to 7 p.m., and once it was all (*to grind*), we put it in sacks and (*to lay*) each sack on the ground outside the mill. Then we all (*to lie*) down and immediately (*to fall*) asleep.

###

D: PUNCTUATION

Entire books have been written about English punctuation. The correct use of punctuation symbols – periods, commas, semicolons, colons, question marks, exclamation marks, apostrophes, dashes, hyphens, parentheses and quotation marks – is a problem for writers the world over, and a matter of heated debate among scholars.

Some grammarians call for extensive use of commas and semicolons; others say commas should be used sparingly, and semicolons should not be used at all. The British and the Americans, typically, can't even agree on what all the symbols should be called. What the Americans call a "period," the British call a "full stop;" the British talk about "inverted commas" while the Americans talk about "quotation marks." It's "parentheses" in American, but "brackets" in British.

Punctuation is too broad a subject to be discussed at length in this small handbook. (For an informative and highly entertaining discussion of punctuation, see the book "*Eats, Shoots & Leaves*" by Lynne Truss [Profile Books 2003]).

However, there are certain points of punctuation that frequently cause problems for people writing English as a second language, and several of these are discussed below.

* * *

Apostrophes and Possessives

* The apostrophe has a number of uses in English.

1. Apostrophes are used to indicate possession, authorship or sponsorship.

   SINGULAR POSSESSIVE: *John's* car = the car owned by John.
   (When the possessor is a singular thing or person, the apostrophe comes *between* the person's name and the "*s*").

PLURAL POSSESSIVE: The *students'* books = the books owned by the students.

(When the possessors are plural – more than one person or thing – the apostrophe comes *after* the "*s*.")

AUTHORSHIP: The *professor's* theory = the theory formulated by the professor.

SPONSORSHIP: *Hong Kong's* favorite actor = the actor most favored by the people of Hong Kong.

EXCEPTION: Possessive pronouns – *his, hers, its, ours, yours and theirs*, along with *oneself* – do *not* take apostrophes.

2. Apostrophes are used to indicate that a letter or letters (or numbers) have been left out. The resulting shorter words are called "*contractions*."

Didn't = did not (*didn't* is a contraction of *did not*)
We'll = we will (*we'll* is a contraction)
The '90s = the 1990s (*'90s* is a contraction)

3. Apostrophes are used in some people's names:

O'Reilly, D'Aguilar

4. Another major function of the apostrophe is to avoid confusion when certain words and letters are made into plurals. Apostrophes, for example, are used to form the plural of individual letters.

"Mind your *p's* and *q's*" is an English expression meaning "Be polite" or "Follow the rules."

Without the apostrophe, this would read, "Mind your *ps* and *qs*," which would be confusing.

5. Some English writing guides say apostrophes should be used to form the plurals of individual words, other guides say they should not. In general, the choice is yours. However, option B below, without the apostrophes, could be confusing to a reader.

OPTION A: "Here are the *do's* and *don't's* of the English language."

OPTION B: "Here are the *dos* and *don'ts* of the English language."

6. Apostrophes *have no place in most common plurals.* A sign advertising "Fresh *vegetable's* for sale" would be bad English.

* ***Two very similar-looking words that cause great confusion***, even among native English speakers, are "*its*" and "*it's.*"

The first, as indicated in the exception to point 1 above, is a possessive pronoun; it refers to something that is owned by "*it*" and it does *not* take an apostrophe.

The second is a contraction of the words "*it is*" or "*it has,*" and it requires an apostrophe to show that letters are missing.

> **WRONG**: The university held *it's* graduation ceremony yesterday.

> **CORRECT**: The university held *its* graduation ceremony yesterday.

> **CORRECT**: The university's graduation ceremony will be held today, and *it's* [it is] going to be a huge event. *It's* [it has] been a long time since *we've* [we have] had one *that's* [that is] quite so elaborate. The administration says it *can't* [cannot] remember when *its* staff has worked so hard on an event.

* Marks that look similar to apostrophes, called "single quotes" or "inside quotes," are used to set off a quotation inside a quotation.

> **EXAMPLE**: "I heard someone shout, '*Help me,*' and then everything was quiet," the rescue worker said.

* * *

Commas and Periods (or Full Stops)

* When inserting a name, a title or a clause in the middle of a sentence, use commas on *both* sides of the insertion, not just on one side.

> **EXAMPLE**: Insert the name "Gordon Brown" in the following sentence:
> "The prime minister said he would run for re-election."

WRONG: "The prime minister, *Gordon Brown* said he would run for re-election (*missing comma after* "*Brown*")."

CORRECT: "The prime minister, *Gordon Brown*, said he would run for re-election (*commas both before and after the inserted name*)."

WRONG: The best way to learn to write *well assuming* you have the time, is to practice daily (*missing comma before* "*assuming*").

CORRECT: The best way to learn to write *well*, assuming you have the *time*, is to practice daily (*commas inserted before* "*assuming*" *and after* "*time*").

* A sentence ends with a *period* (or *full stop*), with a *question mark*, or with an *exclamation point*. A new sentence starts with a capital letter. Many native Chinese speakers incorrectly string together several sentences, separated only by commas, and without capital letters at their start, like this:

A sentence ends with a period, a new sentence starts with a capital letter, many Chinese incorrectly string together...

* Americans use a period after *all* abbreviations of honorifics: Mr. (*an abbreviation of "Mister"*), Mrs., Ms. (*see note below*), Prof. or Dr. The British tend to do it two ways:

1. If the abbreviation ends with the same letter as in the full word, they do not follow the abbreviation by a full stop (*Mr* and *Mister*; *Mrs* and *Missus*; *Dr* and *Doctor*; *Cpl* and *Corporal*). They do not use a full stop after *Ms*, which has no long version.

2. If the abbreviation ends in a different letter from the full word, they do use a full stop (*Prof.* and *Professor*; *Gen.* and *General*)

   NOTE: "Ms." (pronounced "Miz"), a word that came into general use in the 1970s, has no long form. Strictly speaking, it is not an abbreviation, but simply a neutral term invented to identify a woman who is either married ("Missus," "Mrs.") or single ("Miss"), just as "Mr." can refer to either a married or a single man. Nevertheless, the Americans write the word with a period ("*Ms.*"). The British write it without ("*Ms*").

* * *

Quotations and Quotation Marks

* A quotation plus its *attribution* (the person or document that made the statement) together form a single, complete sentence.

"I am leaving now," *he said.*

"We feel the proposed legislation is not in the best interests of the public," *the party's written statement said.*

In both cases, these are single sentences, and since the attributions ("*he said;*" "*the party's written statement said*") are only one part of the complete sentences, the attributions should *not* start with a capital letter. Chinese speakers often write quotes and their attributions incorrectly as two sentences, with a period in between, like this:

WRONG: "I am leaving *now.*" *He* said. (*Period between the quote and the attribution; attribution begins with a capital letter.*)

CORRECT: "I am leaving *now,*" *he* said. (*Comma between the quote and the attribution; attribution begins with a lower-case letter.*)

WRONG: "The economy grew at a rate of 7.5 percent in the last *quarter.*" *The* Chinese Commerce Ministry announced today.

CORRECT: "The economy grew at a rate of 7.5 percent in the last *quarter,*" *the* Chinese Commerce Ministry announced today.

* Where to put the closing punctuation in a quotation is another English-language question that separates Americans and Britons.

Quoted passages, whether they are full sentences or only a few words, are enclosed by what Americans call "quotation marks" and the British call "inverted commas."

In most cases, Americans will put the punctuation that comes at the end of the quoted passage *inside* the closing quotation mark, as in the line above:

*…and the British call **"inverted commas."***

The British, and those schooled in British English – Hong Kong students, for example – routinely place the final punctuation *outside* the closing quotation mark:

*…and the British call **"inverted commas"**.*

According to the authoritative *Economist Style Guide* (www.economist.com/style/), published by the British news magazine *The Economist*, the British style is often used incorrectly. If the quoted sentence ends with a period, a question-mark (or an exclamation mark), the *Economist* guide says, put the punctuation – American style – *inside* the closing quotation mark:

*"I have to go to Guangzhou **tomorrow."***
*"What's the fastest way to go from Hong Kong to **Guangzhou?"***
*"That train was really **fast!"***

When a quoted sentence is followed by an attribution, British writers tend to place a comma outside the closing quotation mark:

*"The fastest way from Hong Kong to Guangzhou is by **train", the tour guide said.***

But the *Economist* guide agrees with the Americans that this comma also belongs *inside* the closing quotation mark:

*"The fastest way from Hong Kong to Guangzhou is by **train," the tour guide said.***

> **WRONG:** "What time is **it**"**?** Shirley asked.
> **CORRECT:** "What time is **it?**" Shirley asked.
>
> **WRONG:** "It's **late**"**,** William said, "and I am going **home**".
> **CORRECT:** "It's **late,**" William said, "and I am going **home.**"
>
> **WRONG:** "I am leaving **now**"**,** he said.
> **CORRECT:** "I am leaving **now,**" he said.

There is little agreement on which style to use when the quoted passage is only a snippet of a sentence, or the title of a book, for example, and therefore contains no punctuation of its own. The general British style in such a case is to put the punctuation *outside* the closing quotation marks:

*In **"Getting it Done"**, a new book published this week…*

American style remains consistent: put the closing punctuation *inside* the closing quotation mark:

*In **"Getting it Done,"** a new book published this week…*

There is Anglo-American agreement in this case: If a quoted passage appears in a question, but the quoted passage *itself* is not a question, then the question mark belongs *outside* the closing quotation mark.

For example, the English phrase **"Mister Right"** refers to the man of a woman's dreams. In the question below, wondering when this ideal lover might be found, the quoted words themselves ("Mister Right") are not a question, so the question mark belongs *outside* the closing quotation mark:

*When, she wondered, would she finally find her **"Mister Right"**?*

* * *

The Hour

* The British and the Americans punctuate the hour differently. The British write, for example, "7.35," with a full stop between the hour and the minutes, while the Americans write "7:35," with a colon.

###

E: ADDITIONAL GRAMMAR PROBLEMS

Prepositions

Prepositions are words that indicate position, direction or time relationship: "to," "from," "in," "at," "on," "under," "over," "before," "after." Which preposition to use in which situation is difficult to learn whenever you go from one language to another. What is "*in*" in one language might be "*on*" in another; what is "*to*" in one language" is "*at*" in another. Once again, the only way to learn the correct use of prepositions is word by word. However, some very general rules can be stated for English prepositions.

1. People or things tend to be "*in*" a country, a city or a region ("I work *in* China;" "I live *in* San Francisco;" "The country is located *in* the Middle East"), but "*at*" a place or an event ("I teach *at* Tsinghua University;" "He became sick while he was *at* the football match"), and "*on*" an island ("I was *on* Phuket when the tsunami struck in 2004;" "My factory is located *on* Taiwan.").

   WRONG: He is studying accounting *in* The University of Hong Kong.

   CORRECT: He is studying accounting *at* The University of Hong Kong.

BEWARE: Prepositions can be tricky. In correct English, you would live "*in* Mainland China," for example, but you would work "*on* the mainland," and you could make a business trip either "*to*" or "*on*" the mainland." People travel "*in*" an airplane or a car, but "*on*" a ship. Things happen "*in*" a particular year or month, but "*on*" a particular day or date ("She was born *on* a Tuesday *in* the year 1990;" "She was born *on* July 4th, 1990.").

2. People or things generally go "*from*" one thing "*to*" another. This includes a change in location ("I drive *from* my house *to* the university five days a week."), a change in quantity or number ("The death toll in the earthquake rose *from* 25 *to* 68 as more bodies were recovered from the rubble."), a range of options ("The car dealer offered everything *from* 10-year-old Hondas *to* brand new Porsches."), or a period in time ("I work *from* 8 a.m. *to* 7 p.m. five days a week.").

Many people incorrectly leave out the preposition "*to*" in a "from-and-to" phrase:

WRONG: "The university will be closed *from October 2-12.*"

CORRECT: "The university will be closed *from* October 2 *to* October 12." (The word "*to*" has to be included between the numbers.)

3. People or things tend to be "*between*" one place or one range "*and*" another: "He lives *between* Guangzhou *and* Shenzhen." It is incorrect to use a hyphen in place of the second preposition, as illustrated below:

WRONG: "The exhibition will be held *between March 15-May 31.*"

CORRECT: "The exhibition will be held *between* March 15 *and* May 31." (The word "*and*" has to be included between the dates if the word "*between*" is used.)

WRONG: "The trip usually takes *between 2 ½–3 hours.*"

CORRECT: "The trip usually takes *between* 2 ½ hours *and* 3 hours;" "The trip ranges *from* 2 ½ *to* 3 hours." (The word "*and*" or "*to*" has to be included.)

4. Many Chinese writers will insert a needless preposition after certain verbs, for example "to request." In the sentence "He requested *for* a passport," the word "*for*" is not needed. It should read "He requested a passport."

Again, prepositions can trick you. No preposition is needed in sentences like "She entered HKU in 2008," or "She left HKU in 2009." But the preposition "*from*" is required when talking about her graduation: "She graduated *from* HKU in 2009."

* * *

Capitalization

The rules for capitalizations differ somewhat from American to British English. The British capitalize nouns more frequently than Americans do. However, many native Chinese speakers go far beyond even the more liberal British rules, capitalizing (incorrectly) almost every noun that appears on the page. Here are some general rules for either British or American English:

1. In general, capitalize only proper names: people (Hu Jintao), countries or cities (Hong Kong), formal organizations (the World Health Organization), companies (Microsoft Corp.), specific geographical entities (the Great Wall of China, the Sahara Desert), streets and roads (Queen's Road, Broadway, the Champs Elysees).

2. In general, capitalize titles *only when they are coupled with the person's name.* Thus, it is "*President* Barack Obama" or "*President* Obama" (the word "President" capitalized). But it is "the *president*" ("president" in lower case) when the title appears without the name. The same goes for "the *prime minister*," "the *dean*," or "the *chief executive*."

   EXAMPLE: I spoke with *President Obama* for an hour today. The *president* told me he was pleased with the progress our department is making.

3. If the name and the title are separated by commas, the title should *not* be capitalized.

   EXAMPLE: He told the Chinese *premier*, Wen Jiabao, that he would not be able to attend the conference in Beijing.

   EXAMPLE: The American *secretary of state*, Hillary Clinton, will deliver a major speech at the United Nations tomorrow.

   EXCEPTION: In British usage, "rough" or partial names are sometimes capitalized. Thus, in formal British usage, it is correct to write "The University of Hong Kong" in the first reference, and "the *University*" (upper case) in later references. Americans would write "the *university*" (lower case) in all later references.

4. In some cases a title is virtually the same as a name. In this case, the title is *always* capitalized: the Agha Khan, the Dalai Lama, the Shah of Iran.

5. As mentioned earlier, when the word "*the*" is a formal part of a name, the word should be capitalized along with the rest of the name: *The* University of Hong Kong, *The* Times of London, *The* South China Morning Post. Otherwise, "*the*" should be in lower case: *the* World Health Organization; *the* Leaning Tower of Pisa, *the* Forbidden City, *the* Hong Kong government.

* * *

"Which" and "That"

This one confuses a lot of people, Britons and Americans, native and non-native English speakers. In order to explain it, let's start with a question: If George Bernard Shaw's famous comment about British and American English were rewritten, which of the two forms below would be correct?

(A) "Great Britain and America are nations *which* are separated by a common language."

(B) "Great Britain and America are nations *that* are separated by a common language."

Here's the rule to determine whether to use "*which*" or "*that*:"

> In sentences (A) and (B) above, the words "*which*" and "*that*" are used to introduce descriptive phrases: "*…which are separated by a common language;*" "*…that are separated by a common language.*"

> If the sentence could stand alone without the descriptive phrase – if the phrase could be deleted without changing the *meaning* or the *understandability* of the sentence – then "*which*" is the correct word to use.

> But if the phrase is needed for the sentence to be understood fully, "*that*" is the correct word.

Take sentence (A) and eliminate the descriptive phrase: you are left with: "Great Britain and America are nations." That's still an understandable sentence, but Shaw's meaning is lost entirely.

So the information *is needed* in the sentence, and a "*that*" phrase (sentence B) is the correct one:

> "Great Britain and America are nations *that* are separated by a common language."

A "*which*" phrase must be separated by commas from the rest of the sentence, while a "*that*" phrase uses no commas. In the correct sentence above (sentence B), there is no comma between the words "*nations*" and "*that*."

To repeat:

DESCRIPTIVE PHRASE NEEDED: use "*that*."
DESCRIPTIVE PHRASE NOT NEEDED: use "*which*," set phrase off with commas.

EXAMPLE #1: The big house, *which has a red roof*, is going to be torn down tomorrow.

EXPLANATION: There is only one house involved here, and it is going to be torn down. The color of its roof makes no difference. The phrase "*…which has a red roof…*" is a description that is *not* needed for the sentence to be understood. If the phrase is deleted, the remaining sentence ("*The house…is going to be torn down tomorrow*") is still perfectly understandable and conveys the full original meaning.

Therefore, **DESCRIPTIVE PHRASE NOT NEEDED**: "*Which*" is the correct word here, and the phrase is set off by commas.

EXAMPLE #2: A building contractor receives a work order that reads as follows: "The house *that has a red roof* must be torn down tomorrow, but all the other houses must be left standing."

EXPLANATION: In this case, the contractor has a lot of houses to choose from. Only the descriptive phrase "*…that has a red roof…*" makes it clear which specific house he is to tear down. If the phrase is deleted from the sentence, the contractor will have no way of knowing which of the many houses he is supposed to tear down; he might demolish the wrong one.

Therefore, **DESCRIPTIVE PHRASE NEEDED**: "*That*" is the correct choice here, and there are no commas.

NOTE: A lot of British and Australian writers reverse the rule, and use "*which*" in place of "*that*." It might be common practice, but it's still bad English.

###

CHAPTER FOUR
Bits and Pieces

Here are some miscellaneous elements of English that often cause trouble for writers. Like the distinction between "*which*" and "*that*," these points can lead to mistakes even among native English speakers.

The prefix "re"

The prefix "*re*" can be inserted in front of almost any verb, and it usually means "*to do again*:"

> Reappear = To appear again
> Reassess = To assess again
> Repossess = To possess again, to take possession again

However, putting a "*re*" in front of a verb that starts with the letter "*e*" can lead to confusion about how the word should be pronounced:

> Elect – *Reelect*
> Evaluate – *Reevaluate*
> Enter – *Reenter*

To avoid confusion, in verbs that start with the letter "*e*," a hyphen is usually inserted after the "*re*:"

> Elect – *Re-elect*
> Evaluate – *Re-evaluate*
> Enter – *Re-enter*

In addition, some verbs already start with the letters "*re*," such as "*recover*." And "*recover*" in this case does not mean "*to cover again*;" it means to "*regain something that was lost or taken*." To avoid confusion, the verb "*to cover again*" should be written with a hyphen:

> To regain something lost – *Recover*
> To cover something again - *Re-cover*

The same goes for such verbs as "*reform*" (to improve, to change to a better state) and "*re-form*" (to form again); or "*reflex*" (an involuntary reaction) and "*re-flex*" (to flex again).

The prefix "*re*" can also be put in front of a noun, as in "*recombination*" or "*recalculation*," and again it refers to something being done again. But there can also be confusion here, because some nouns also already start with the letters "*re*." Take, for example, the word "*recreation*:" does it mean "*something that was created again*," or does it mean "*enjoyment*"?

In fact, it means both. It's easy to tell the two meanings apart when the words are spoken, because they're pronounced differently: the word meaning "*enjoyment*" is pronounced "REK-ree-ay-shun," while "*something created again*" is pronounced "REE-KREE-ay-shun." To avoid confusion between the *written* words, it's best to write the word for "*something created again*" with a hyphen:

> Enjoyment, pleasure – *Recreation*
> Something created again – *Re-creation*

The important thing in a situation like this is to ask yourself whether there might be confusion in understanding or pronouncing a new word when the prefix "*re*" is added. If the meaning you want to convey is "*to do something again*," then using "*re-*" with a hyphen is an effective and grammatically acceptable way to ensure there is no confusion.

* * *

"Percent" vs. "Percentage points"

Business writing, which is very important in today's world, frequently requires reference to numbers, such as prices, amounts and percentages. A point that often trips up even good writers is the difference between "a *percent*" and "a *percentage point*."

The difference is very real, and if you confuse the two – in a letter to a customer, or in a news story, for example – it can lead to a serious error. To say, "The import duty on this item has been increased by 5 *percent*" is *very different* from saying, "The import duty on this item has been increased by 5 *percentage points*." This small difference in wording can lead to a large difference in dollars.

This difference can also be explained with an illustration:

Let us say that your company in China is shipping goods worth $1,000 to a company in the United States, and the existing import duty on the goods – the tax your customer has to pay the U.S. government to bring the item into the country – is 15%:

This is an increase of 5 *percent* in the existing duty:

Existing duty rate:	15%
Existing duty on $1,000:	15% of $1,000 = (.15 x 1,000) = $150
5 percent increase in duty:	5% of $150 = (.05 x 150) = $7.50
Original duty plus 5 percent	$150 + $7.50 = $157.50

The original duty was $150. The original duty has been increased by **5 percent**. The new duty is $157.50. Your customer is paying $7.50 more than he paid before.

This is an increase of 5 *percentage points* in the existing duty:

Existing duty rate:	15%
Existing duty on $1,000:	15% of $1,000 = .15 x 1,000 = $150
Each whole *percent* = one *percentage point*:	15% = 15 percentage points
Increase of 5 percentage points in duty:	15 + 5 = 20
New duty rate:	20%
New duty on $1,000:	20% of $1,000 = (.20 x 1,000) = $200

The original duty was $150. The duty rate has been increased by **5 percentage points**, from 15 to 20 percent. The new duty is $200. *Your customer is paying* **$50** *more than he paid before.*

* * *

"Farther" and "Further"

These two are routinely confused. "Farther" refers to increased distance, while "further" refers to additional quantity or time.

"To reach the main highway, drive 2 kilometers *farther* (distance) along this road, and then turn west at the intersection."

"I read a hundred pages *farther* (*distance*) into the book and I still didn't find the information I was looking for."

"We're going to need *further* (*quantity*) volunteers if we want to have any chance of finishing the project on time."

"I'm getting tired. I'm going to read a bit *further* (*time*), and then I'm going to go to sleep."

* * *

"Less" and "Fewer"

"Less" is used with things that cannot be divided. "Fewer" is used with things that can be counted individually.

"There's been *less sunshine* this month than last month." ("*Sunshine*" is indivisible; a person cannot count individual "*sunshines*.")

"There is *less water* in the tank than there was yesterday."

"We have *less time* to complete the project than we thought we had."

"We have *fewer days* to complete the project than we thought we had." ("*Days*" can be counted individually.)

"There are *fewer boys* than girls in our class."

"Every day, our *chances* of success become *fewer and fewer.*"

* * *

"Even"

Native Chinese speakers often incorrectly use the word "*even*" in place of the word "*also*." In correct usage, "*even*" usually indicates that something unusual or excessive has taken place. Or, it can be used to give extra emphasis to "more than" or "less than."

WRONG: "He put on his pants, and he *even* put on his shoes." (There is nothing unusual about a man putting on his shoes, so "*even*" is the wrong choice here.)

CORRECT: "He put on his pants, and he *also* put on his shoes."

CORRECT: "She read every book on the subject she could find, she studied on the weekends, and she *even* took a cram course, but she still failed the exam." (In this case, the word "*even*" indicates that taking a cram course involved greater-than-normal effort, so "*even*" is correct here.)

CORRECT: "The number of car accidents in October was higher than normal for this time of year, and *even higher* than during the busy summer months."

CORRECT: "Because of the recession, we have *even fewer* customers on the weekends than we normally have during the week."

* * *

"Besides"

Native Chinese speakers often incorrectly use the word "*besides*" where they should use "*in addition*" or "*also*" or "*in the meantime*."

WRONG: He is going to major in accounting at the university. *Besides*, he is going to take some courses in art history.

CORRECT: He is going to major in accounting at the university. *In addition*, he is going to take some courses in art history.

WRONG: They were practicing every day for the university singing competition. *Besides*, they were studying for their final exams.

CORRECT: They were practicing every day for the university singing competition. *In the meantime*, they were *also* studying for their final exams.

* * *

"Comprise," "Compose," "Constitute"

These three words have similar meanings, but they are used quite differently in a sentence. To "comprise" is "*to include,*" "*to embrace.*" To "compose" is "*to form,*" "*to make* (into a thing)." To "constitute" also means to make into a thing, but it is used differently from "compose," as shown in the examples below.

1. The orchestra is *composed* [is made] of several different sections: the strings, the woodwinds, the brass and the percussion.

2. The strings, the woodwinds, the brass and the percussion *constitute* [form] the orchestra.

3. The orchestra *comprises* [includes] the strings, the woodwinds, the brass and the percussion.

###

CHAPTER FIVE

Tips for writing effective press releases, public notices and business letters

People write for many different audiences (in this case, the plural of the word "*audience*" is the correct choice). You might write to a customer, in an e-mail containing the details of a shipment. Your might write to a client, with a financial analysis of a company the client is thinking of investing in. You might write a memo to your colleagues or business associates. You might write to capture the attention of a journalist, as in a press release. You might write for the general public, as in a newspaper story, or to announce an upcoming cultural performance to people who might want to attend.

There are certain rules for writing such things effectively, and these are discussed below. In addition, in all cases, if you want your writing to be effective, you have to keep in mind all the rules and the points of grammar discussed above. Keep reminding yourself that your purpose is communication: you will not communicate anything if your writing is unintelligible, badly organized, and full of jargon and irrelevant information.

A lot of people think writing has to be long in order to be good. Others think their writing will only be respected if it is full of academic or technical terminology. They are wrong. People don't respect writing that is overblown or difficult to understand. On the contrary, when they see such writing, they're likely to toss it away without reading it. Instead of communicating, the writer has wasted his time.

This section makes reference to the rules of good writing that are listed at the start of this booklet. And one of the first rules is, always keep your audience in mind. That means more than just identifying who your target audience is. It also means keeping the audience's needs and circumstances in mind. Along with that, you should always keep in mind what *the purpose* of your writing is.

In other words, before you write, make sure you understand three things:

    (1) whom you are aiming at;
    (2) the best way to reach that person or group; and
    (3) what you want your writing to accomplish.

EXAMPLE: You work in the public relations office of a large company, and you want the news media to write about the company's latest product. You write a press release, which describes the product and invites reporters to attend a press conference at which the product will be introduced and explained. What should you keep in mind while you're writing?

The target audience of your press release (point 1 above) is journalists – the editors who assign stories, the reporters who cover and write stories. Your goal (point 3) is to persuade those journalists to send someone to your press conference and write about your company's accomplishment.

In order to achieve this - in order to reach your target with an effective communication (point 2) – there are several things you should do:

    * **Keep your audience in mind**. Journalists are busy people, working under daily and even hourly deadlines. They are bombarded every day by notices from corporations and institutions and individuals who want to see their ideas or accomplishments reported in the news media. A journalist doesn't have the time to read through a long, complicated press release, or to try to figure out what a badly written press release means to say. Therefore:

    * **Get to the point**. Tell the journalists right away, in the opening sentence, what the press release is all about; tell them right away what the most important information is. Also, and this is especially important if you want your press release to be effective: make it sound interesting enough that it will catch their eye among all the other press releases they've received that day.

If your organization has taken a public opinion poll and come up with some interesting results, the opening sentence of the press release should tell what those results are. Remember this rule: the "news" – the information that's of interest to the public and that's going to attract a journalist's attention – is *not* that a public opinion poll was held; the news is what the public opinion poll *discovered*.

In early 2010, the Chinese University of Hong Kong conducted a poll to measure the Hong Kong public's views on government proposals for democratic reform. This is an issue that had been debated actively in Hong Kong for many years. Public opinion on this important subject was something the public would be interested in hearing about. Yet here's the first part of a press release on the subject that was published on the university's website:

Second Opinion Poll on 2012 Constitutional Reforms

A Forum on 'Constitutional Reform in Hong Kong: Where Do We Go?' was held at The Chinese University of Hong Kong (CUHK) today. The organizer of the forum, Hong Kong Institute of Asia-Pacific Studies (HKIAPS), CUHK, released the findings of the second opinion poll on 2012 constitutional reforms.

The second telephone survey was conducted from 28 January to 4 February 2010, and successfully interviewed 1,009 respondents aged 18 or above. The results of statistical analysis were weighted according to the Hong Kong population statistics in mid-2009 published by the Census and Statistics Department.

The second opinion poll finds that slightly more than half (51.2%) of the respondents support the Government's proposal on the 2012 constitutional reforms. As the consultation period for the constitutional reforms will soon come to an end, the research team still maintains its previous position that the Government lacks a very strong foundation to push forward the current proposal. In fact, *more than 60% of respondents do not agree that the Government has made the best proposal under current circumstances*.

First of all, the headline in this press release tells the reader next to nothing: it just hints that a poll was taken. Second, the text devotes the first two paragraphs – the first 10 lines of copy – to telling the reader (a) that a forum was held, and (b) who organized the forum (including some very long initials), and (c) that at the forum, the results of a poll were released, and (d) when and how the poll was taken, and (e) how the results were "weighted."

It's not until the third paragraph that the press release finally gets to the point: 51.2% of the public supports the government's proposal, but more than 60% say the government hasn't made the best proposal.

That important information should have been in the very first sentence of the press release. Instead, it was buried amid some long-winded and unimportant information. Is the average person reading this press release even likely to understand the meaning of "*The results of statistical analysis were weighted according to the Hong Kong population statistics in mid-2009 published by the Census and Statistics Department*"? Probably not. That's opinion-poll jargon, and another of the rules of good writing is that jargon should be avoided. But the reader had to fight his way past that jargon-filled sentence and several others before finding out what the press release was all about.

So keep the purpose of your press release in mind, and write it accordingly.

Your organization has made a major breakthrough in medical research? Don't bury that all-important information. Tell the journalists right at the start: "We've created a drug that's going to cure tens of thousands of people." That will get their attention.

Here's another example of an ineffective press release: In early 2010, the Chinese University medical school announced that it had developed an easy test for predicting whether certain people might contract liver cancer. That's a pretty important development, especially for people in the high-risk group. But here's the way the CUHK website handled the announcement:

CUHK Developed a Simple Score to Predict Future Risk of Liver Cancer in Patients with Chronic Hepatitis B

Around 500,000 people in Hong Kong suffer from chronic hepatitis B, among whom 25% eventually die of liver cancer or cirrhotic complications. Screening ultrasound and alfa-fetoprotein testing every 6 to 12 months is recommended to pick up early liver cancer. Anti-viral treatment that suppresses hepatitis B virus can reduce the risk of liver cancer. However, most patients may require long-term anti-viral treatment. The large number of patients in the community has imposed a heavy burden to the health resources on cancer screening and hepatitis treatment. A tool that can provide accurate assessment of cancer risk will be important to guide the optimal use of healthcare resources.

The Department of Clinical Oncology and Department of Medicine and Therapeutics of The Chinese University of Hong Kong (CUHK) *have jointly developed and validated a simple score to predict the risk of liver cancer in patients with chronic hepatitis B* by conducting a 10-year study. *This new score can identify and prioritize high-risk patients for regular liver cancer surveillance and anti-viral treatment."*

This time, at least, the headline on the website did tell what the press release was all about. But to locate the details, a reader had to wade through a 10-line-long first paragraph filled with medical terminology like "*cirrhotic complications*" and "*alfa-fetoprotein testing.*" The important news – that a new test had been devised – was buried in the middle of a second long paragraph, surrounded by a lot more big words: "*developed and validated,*" "*identify and prioritize…for…surveillance and anti-viral treatment.*"

The first paragraph of this press release *should* have read like this:

"A new and simple test to predict the risk of liver cancer in patients with chronic hepatitis B has been devised by researchers at the Chinese University of Hong Kong."

That's it. Thirty words instead of the 152 words it took the original press release to get to the point.

What else should someone writing a press release keep in mind?

* **Keep it simple**. Don't load up the press release with every single fact you have about the new product. Save the technical details for the press conference. In the press release, just include the highlights, enough to pique the journalist's interest and show that the event is important enough for him to spend his company's time on. In the two examples above, if all that detail needs to be in the press release at all, it should be at the bottom – *after* the important information has been given.

* **Make it understandable**. It goes without saying that the grammar, spelling and vocabulary in your press release should be correct, so the journalist can understand what you're trying to tell him. (A badly written press release will give the impression that your company is not professional. In that case, the journalist may decide it is not worth spending the time to attend your press conference.) But more than grammar and spelling are important.

* **Leave the jargon out of the press release**. The journalists you're sending the press release to are probably not biologists, or chemists, or medical doctors; they probably won't understand terms like "*alfa-fetaprotein testing*." Instead of loading up the press release with scientific and medical terms, use terms that the average person can understand. If you do refer to something technical in the press release, make sure you explain it – but leave most of the science for the experts at the press conference to explain.

* **Avoid hyperbole**. Don't overstate the case. If your company really has developed a cure for a major disease, that's an important accomplishment and you are entitled to brag about it. But don't overdo it. Don't try to make it sound bigger than it really is. Don't make claims for the product that aren't supported by the facts.

If the discovery is truly important, just list the facts in a straightforward and understandable way, and the situation will speak for itself. That's the way to get a message across to a journalist.

* * *

How do you translate all these rules, then, into a well-written and effective press release? Let's go through the procedure step by step.

First, consider how to organize your press release. Journalists use a four-part structure to organize their news stories. Press releases are usually shorter than news stories (at least they should be), but the same basic structure should be used to make sure the press release delivers the necessary information in brief, simple and understandable form. Here are the four parts:

Part 1 - The lead.

This is the opening paragraph, the one that "leads" off the story or press release. It tells the reader, in a nutshell, what has happened, or what is going to happen. The lead should contain the most important information, and *only* the most important information. In our sample case, the most important information is that (A) your company has developed an important new cure for a major disease, and (B) a press conference is going to be held at which the drug will be explained to the public. That's the information that belongs in the lead.

Part 2 – One or more paragraphs that support, explain and amplify the lead.

The paragraphs that immediately follow the lead should support the lead with hard facts, explanations of terms, and details that are missing in the lead.

Part 3 – Any important background or context.

Sometimes, there's some history involved in the situation that needs to be explained. You might need to explain, for example, that it took 10 years of research before the new drug could be developed, and it has gone through several test trials to make sure it is safe and effective. That kind of "background" information belongs in this third section.

Sometimes, there are other factors that have an impact on your announcement. This drug might have been rushed to market more quickly than normal, for example, in an attempt to halt an outbreak of a dangerous new disease, like the swine flu outbreak of 2009-2010. That information puts the announcement "into context" for the reader.

Background and context can appear anywhere in the press release *after the lead*. The point is not to add extra words, but to make sure that you have left no unanswered questions and omitted no important points.

Part 4 - Additional information

This is where to add information that is not important enough for the beginning of the press release, but which helps to tell the full story. Full details of date, time and place of the press conference, for example, could be placed here. If the press release announces the appointment of a person to a new position, the person's biography might go here. If some highly technical terms are necessary in the press release, they can be explained here.

Now let's see how this four-step structure is put to use in different types of writing for public consumption.

* * *

Press Releases

Below are a couple of sets of sample facts (they are based on real situations, but some names and dates have been changed). We'll write press releases from these facts, using the rules of good writing and the four-step structure.

Fact sheet #1. The following facts were all included in a press release issued by The University of Hong Kong Libraries in early 2010:

1. Dr. Liu Yandong is a member of the Chinese State Council.

2. She visited the HKU campus in December 2009, and said the university, with its wealth of experience in grooming talent and pioneering research, is well placed to support China's efforts to improve education standards and acquire advanced international educational concepts.

3. She has donated a set of the *Yongle Dadian*, the Ming Dynasty-era Chinese encyclopedia, to The University of Hong Kong Libraries.

4. The *Yongle Dadian* was compiled between 1403 and 1407, during the reign of the Yongle Emperor. It is considered to be the longest encyclopedia ever compiled.

5. The aim of the project was to compile everything important ever written about Chinese history, philosophy, the arts, sciences, and the Confucian canon, up to that point.

6. The original encyclopedia included 23,000 manuscript scrolls divided into 11,095 volumes. Only three copies of the work were ever made in manuscript form, and the first two have disappeared or were destroyed.

7. Fewer than 400 of the volumes have survived into modern times. The most complete edition is the 163-volume set in the National Library of China, which is located in Beijing. The edition donated by Ms. Liu is a facsimile of that set.

8. A ceremony to mark Ms. Liu's donation and to display the encyclopedia will be held on Wednesday, 3 March 2010, at 4:00 p.m. on the ground floor of the new wing of the HKU Main Library. The encyclopedia will

be available for detailed viewing after the ceremony, and members of the library staff will be available to answer questions about it.

9. HKU Vice-Chancellor Lap-chee Tsui and a representative of the Liaison Office of the Central People's Government will officiate jointly at the ceremony.

10. Those interested in attending or wishing further information should contact Ms Sally Wong, HKU Libraries (Tel: 2859-2211).

Analysis of the facts. You now have the facts, you're ready to write. First, ask yourself some questions:

1. **What is the purpose of this press release?**
Answer: to inform reporters of this important donation, and to persuade them to attend and write about the donation ceremony and the encyclopedia itself. Therefore, information regarding those two key points should form the lead paragraphs of the press release, and the paragraphs should be written so as to make the situation sound as interesting as possible.

2. **Do any items have to be explained?**
Answer: The *Yongle Dadian* is not well known to the average person (including the average reporter). In order for journalists to understand the importance and rarity of the encyclopedia, the press release has to explain its history and what it is.

3. **What else would catch a journalist's eye?**
Answer: Make sure the journalists understand that they will be able to examine the encyclopedia: if they're going to write about it, they're going to want to see it for themselves and ask questions about it. Also, the fact that the Liaison Office of the central government is sending a representative is an indication of how significant the government and the university consider this donation. Journalists are more likely to write a story if it has political significance, so the fact of the Liaison Office's participation should also be near the top of the press release.

4. **What other important facts should be prominently noted?**
Answer: The time, date and location of the ceremony should be written simply and clearly for the journalists' easy reference, and a contact person should be identified in case a journalist has questions.

Finished Product. Here, in four relatively short paragraphs, is what the release should look like:

26 February 2010

Chinese Official Donates Copy of Extremely Rare Chinese Encyclopedia to University of Hong Kong Library

Ceremony and private press viewing to be held Wednesday, 3 March at HKU Library

Information: Sally Wong, HKU Libraries, Tel. 2859-2211, email s.wu@hkul.hku.hk.

A copy of the exceedingly rare *Yongle Dadian*, the vast Chinese encyclopedia compiled during the Ming Dynasty, has been donated to The University of Hong Kong by Dr. Liu Yandong, a member of the Chinese State Council.

Members of the news media are invited to inspect the encyclopedia and attend a ceremony to mark the donation, which will be held on Tuesday, March 3, 2010, in the main library of the university. A representative of the Liaison Office of the Central People's Government will officiate at the ceremony alongside HKU Vice-Chancellor Lap-chee Tsui. Members of the library staff will be on hand to answer journalists' questions about the encyclopedia.

The *Yongle Dadian* was compiled between 1403 and 1408 during the reign of the Yongle Emperor. Originally containing almost 23,000 manuscript scrolls divided into 11,095 volumes, it is considered the longest encyclopedia ever compiled, and was designed to encompass everything important written up to that time on Chinese history, philosophy, the arts, science, and the Confucian canon.

Only three copies of the entire encyclopedia were made, and fewer than 400 volumes have survived into modern times. The most complete existing set is the 163-volume set housed at the National Library of China in Beijing. The edition donated to the HKU Libraries is a facsimile of that set.

Date: Wednesday, 3 March 2010
Time: 4 p.m.
Venue: Ground floor, new wing, Main Library, The University of Hong Kong

Any additional facts – about Ms. Liu, her comments on her prior visit, the encyclopedia and the donation – can be given out at the press conference itself.

* * *

Fact sheet #2. Sometimes a press release is sent out after an event has happened, to alert the news media in case they want to write about it, and as a notice to the public. In this case, since the event has already taken place, there will be no press conference at which the full facts will be given out, so the press release itself has to contain enough information for a full story to be written.

Even so, the press release cannot be too long or too complicated, or it will be ignored. The rules cited in the first example – keep your audience in mind, keep your purpose in mind, get to the point – should all be followed if the press release is to have any chance of being effective.

1. Professor Roland T. Chin was appointed deputy vice-chancellor and provost of The University of Hong Kong on 26 January 2010.

2. He will officially start his five-year term on 1 March 2010, and will serve as the chief aide to Vice-Chancellor Lap-chee Tsui.

3. Professor Chin currently holds the titles of vice-president for academic affairs, deputy president, and chair professor of computer science at the Hong Kong University for Science and Technology.

4. Professor Chin was born in Macau, grew up in Hong Kong, and studied electrical engineering at the University of Missouri in the United States. He subsequently worked at the NASA Goddard Space Flight Center in the state of Maryland, before joining the Faculty of Electrical and Computer Engineering at the University of Wisconsin at Madison, where he served from 1981 to 1995.

5. He joined the Hong Kong University of Science and Technology in 1992 on a part-time basis. He began full-time work and served as a head of department from 1998 to 200. He was seconded to the Hong Kong government's Applied Science and Technology Research Institute as vice president for information technology from 2001 to 2003, then returned to HKUST and served as vice president for research and development from 2003 to 2006.

6. He has won numerous awards in the areas of computer vision, digital image processing and pattern recognition. He has spearheaded the move at HKUST to "reinvent undergraduate education" for the transformation from a three-year to a four-year curriculum. He advocates well-rounded learning experience with flexible curricula, interdisciplinary education, critical thinking and leadership development, global outlook, and out-of-classroom learning experiences.

7. He is a member of the Hong Kong government's University Grants Committee, the Steering Committee on Innovation and Technology and the Commission on Strategic Development, and chairman of the Research Grants Council. He also serves on the board of HKUST's Nano and Advanced Materials Institute and the

Logistics and Supply Chain Management Institute, and as the board chairman of Hong Kong Education City.

8. The appointment was announced by Dr Leong Che-hung, chairman of the HKU Council. "As the University moves into its second century, there will be big challenges ahead. The Hong Kong higher education sector is at a very critical stage of change, with challenges from the introduction of the new 3-3-3-4 education system in 2012, and the move towards increased engagement with the Mainland and the international community," Dr. Leong said. "I believe the vice-chancellor and Professor Chin, together with all other members of the university senior management, will work as a team to successfully fulfill the strategic goals of the University."

9. The appointment was welcomed by Vice-Chancellor Tsui. "As the university continues to reach out and engage the world, Professor Roland Chin's distinguished academic achievements and rich experience in administration and public service made him a most suitable candidate," Prof. Tsui said. "I very much look forward to working in partnership with him to bring the university to new heights of academic excellence and international renown as one of the world's leading institutions of higher learning."

10. Professor Chin said on accepting the appointment: "I am very honoured that the Council, the vice-chancellor, the staff and the students have entrusted me with their confidence in joining the university senior management to take HKU to even greater heights of excellence. I am looking forward to working with the students and the staff to help HKU become one of the premier world-class universities."

11. Professor Chin will succeed Professor Yue-Chim Richard Wong. Professor Wong is retiring.

* * *

Analysis. There's a large amount of material here, and including all these facts in the press release would make it far too long. You have to decide which facts the public would be interested in, perhaps throw in a few abbreviated quotes, and discard the rest.

Identify your audience: this press release is aimed at the general public, but particularly at anyone interested in higher education. To reach that audience, the information should be posted on the HKU and HKUST websites. It should be sent to the websites of other universities and educational institutes. It should be sent to the student newspapers and radio stations on the various campuses. It should be sent as a press release to the news media.

Put the most important information – the fact of the appointment, what Chin will do, when he will start doing it, and what he's been doing up to now – at the top of the press release. Those are the only things most people will want to know. Chin's biography should follow. A few selected quotes from the parties involved may or may not be used by any publication outside HKU (they are routine comments that could have been written by anybody, and almost certainly will not be used by any newspapers), but they should be added at the bottom of the press release just in case anyone wants to use them.

Final product. This one is nine paragraphs long, but *the key information* is loaded into the first three short paragraphs:

Press Release

Roland T. Chin Named New HKU Deputy Vice-Chancellor and Provost

Information: Elsie Tsui, HKU Communications and Public Affairs Office
Tel 2859-2606 email etsui@hku.hk.

(26 January 2010) - Professor Roland T. Chin, a renowned academician and expert in the technological sciences, has been appointed by The University of Hong Kong as deputy vice-chancellor and provost, the HKU Council announced today.

Prof. Chin's five-year term as chief aide to HKU Vice-Chancellor Lap-chee Tsui will officially begin on 1 March. He succeeds Professor Yue-Chim Richard Wong, who is retiring.

Professor Chin currently holds the titles of vice-president for academic affairs, deputy president, and chair professor of computer science, at the Hong Kong University of Science and Technology (HKUST).

Roland T. Chin was born in Macau and grew up in Hong Kong. He studied electrical engineering at the University of Missouri in the United States, worked at the NASA Goddard Space Flight Center in the state of Maryland from 1979 to 1981, then joined the faculty of Electrical and Computer Engineering at the University of Wisconsin at Madison until 1995.

He joined HKUST on a part-time basis in 1992, and served as a head of department there from 1996 to 2000. He was seconded to the Hong Kong government's Applied Science and Technology Research Institute as vice president for information technology from 2001 to 2003, then returned to HKUST as vice president for research and development from 2003 to 2006.

He has served on the Hong Kong government's University Grants Committee, the Steering Committee on Innovation and Technology, and the Commission on Strategic Development, and is board chairman of Hong Kong Education City. He also serves on the board of HKUST's Nano and Advanced Materials Institute and Logistics and Supply Chain Management Institute. He has won numerous awards in the areas of computer vision, digital image processing and pattern recognition.

Announcing the appointment today, HKU Council Chairman Dr Leong Che-hung noted the challenges facing Hong Kong universities, including the four-year curriculum to be introduced in 2012. "I believe the vice-chancellor and Professor Chin, together with all other members of the university senior management, will work as a team to successfully fulfill the strategic goals of the university," Dr. Leong said.

Vice-chancellor Tsui welcomed the appointment. "As the University continues to reach out and engage the world, Professor Roland Chin's distinguished academic achievements and rich experience in administration and public service made him a most suitable candidate," he said.

Prof. Chin expressed pleasure at the opportunity "to take HKU to even greater heights of excellence. I am looking forward to working with the students and the staff to help HKU become one of the premier world-class universities," he said.

* * *

Public Notices

Sometimes, you want to reach a public audience directly, without going through the news media. Perhaps there's going to be an interesting speech, or a musical performance, and you want to invite the general public. You might post a notice on your website. You might also send the notice to other websites – sites that deal with music and musical performances, for example – and ask those sites to post the notice. You might mail out fliers, or post them on walls and signboards so that people will see them as they walk by.

Once again, remember your purpose: to tell people that a performance is going to take place, and invite them to attend. Keep the notice brief and to the point, and make sure the information your audience will want to know is prominently displayed: who is going to do what, where and when it is going to happen, and where tickets can be obtained.

Fact sheet #3. In 2010, a 630-word notice of an upcoming piano recital was posted on a Hong Kong University website. The notice told about the recital, it described the artist's career, background and who her teachers were at length, it quoted press reviews of her albums, and it quoted her personal philosophy. What follows is just *a portion* of what was included in the press release:

The University of Hong Kong is pleased to announce that renowned British-Chinese pianist Evelyn Chang will give a piano recital at Loke Yew Hall on 4 February 2010 at 7:30pm…

Evelyn Chang made her London debut in 2004 at the South Bank Centre…Her 2007 recording with violist Maxim Rysanov released by Avie Records received many awards and was picked as editor's choice by Gramophone, BBC Music and Musik Magazines…

…She was invited to perform at Buckingham Palace at the age of 17. Chang later joined the Royal College of Music, studying under professors Irina Zaritskaya and Andrew Ball, supported by the Russell Gandler Award and St. Martyn's scholarship. She currently resides in Hong Kong under the government's Quality Migrant Scheme.

…Chang will perform selected works by Chopin and Schumann to celebrate the bicentenary of their birth. Limited seats are available for the public. Admission is free. Register at: www.hku.hk/music/concerts/0910_2/piano or enquire at the HKU Department of Music, Tel: 2859 7045…

…Chang's debut solo album, 'Poets from the East,' was released by Avie Records in May 2009. The album has been warmly received by the press and public, and was followed by a series of launch recitals in Asia…

Aside from being a solo and chamber musician, she is also a great champion of contemporary music, actively involved in promoting new music and working closely with composers, some of whose works are…dedicated to her. She also…contributes…to … charities in the UK and Asia…

Originally from Taiwan, encouraged by her teacher Mary Kuok Chiu Tse, she moved to London at the age of 13 and began to explore her long musical journey in the west. During her time at the Purcell School of Music, she regularly gave concerts throughout Europe and the UK under the supervision of Valéria Szervánszky, Graham Fitch and Andrej Esterházy…

Evelyn believes that music has no boundaries. She expresses…from the standard classical repertoire through contemporary music to improvisations…She continuously seeks… new music and new ways to express as an artist…

Analysis. *Eighty-five percent of the above information should not appear* in a public notice. Very few people would bother to read it all. Who cares who the artist's teachers were? Who cares which scholarships she received? Most people just want to hear good music. The rest of the information would be of interest only to devoted fans of the artist, and most of that belongs in the printed program that will be handed out at the concert – not in a notice inviting the general public to attend the concert.

Final product. Here's the way this notice should be written, in three short paragraphs – 86 words instead of the original 630:

Evelyn Chang Piano Recital to Celebrate Bicentenary of Chopin and Schumann

Renowned British-Chinese pianist Evelyn Chang will give a public piano recital at The University of Hong Kong's Loke Yew Hall on Thursday, 4 February 2010, at 7:30 p.m.

Chang, who has released many critically acclaimed albums and has played at Buckingham Palace, will perform selected works by Chopin and Schumann to celebrate the bicentenary of the two composers' births.

Admission is free, but there are limited seats for the public. You may register for tickets at www.hku.hk/music/concerts/0910_2/piano, or contact the HKU Department of Music at 2859-7045.

* * *

Business Letters

There are many types of business letters. The Internet is full of websites with templates for such letters, and if your English is not perfect, these can be a big help in writing to your business contacts.

> **SOME OF THE MANY WEBSITES** offering business letter templates:
> www.writinghelp-central.com
> www.business-letters.org
> www.4hb.com

Again, whatever kind of letter you're writing and whoever your contact is, it's important to keep the main points in mind: write clearly, write simply, make sure your grammar and spelling are correct, make sure your choice of words is good, make sure there are no factual errors in the letter (errors can cost businesses money), and get to the point. Your business associates, just like the journalists you might send press releases to, are busy people. They don't have time to read an encyclopedia; they just want the basic facts from you:

* *Have you shipped their order*? When did it leave and when will it arrive? How was it shipped? What is the waybill number? Who is the shipper's contact?

* *Do you have a new item to offer them*? What is it, what does it do, how is it better than the one they've been using, and how much does it cost?

* *Have you raised your prices*? What are the new prices? Did you include a price list? When do the new prices take effect?

When you write to a business contact, make the tone of the letter appropriate to the information. If the person is a long-time associate or customer, make the letter friendly; make it formal if it's a request for payment or a reference to a legal agreement. In any case, make sure it is absolutely clear and absolutely accurate, and keep it as brief as possible.

Here's an example of a letter announcing price increases:

(Your company's letterhead stationery)

Date:

Addressee

Mailing Address

Dear XXX:

Due to the recent increases in the cost of raw materials, we are forced to raise the retail prices of our merchandise.

We have avoided this for as long as possible, and we have kept the increases as small as possible, but we can no longer delay the inevitable.

Our new price list is enclosed. The new prices will go into effect on (XXX date). Any orders received between now and that date will be honored at our current, lower prices.

We thank you for your continued business and we hope that you will understand the necessity for these increases.

Sincerely,

(signature)

Sales Manager

###

CHAPTER SIX
Real-life Examples of Bad English

Here are some real-life examples of the kind of garbled English that important individuals, government departments, political parties and other prominent figures in this part of the world are regularly guilty of. Many of the types of errors that are discussed in the first five sections of this booklet are illustrated here, along with the author's comments. Mistakes or examples of poor English are written in italics:

Example #1. A partial transcript of English-language remarks by the financial secretary of Hong Kong, John C. Tsang, on February 27, 2010, at a media session after he appeared on a radio programme to discuss the 2010-2011 Hong Kong budget. This transcript appeared on the Hong Kong government website:

Reporter: Are you saying that you already have some measures in mind to tackle the problem that professional investors may change their targets to the mass residential property market after you have raised the stamp duty?

Financial Secretary: We've *push* out a basket of measures already, and we do have other *measure ready, in depending* on the situation *how it evolves*. I think we are already quite determined to ensure our property market proceeds in a stable and healthy manner.

Comments: Bad English from a very high-ranking government official. It should be "we've (we have) *pushed*," present perfect tense. It should be "*measures*," plural. "*In depending on…how it evolves*" is poor syntax.

* * *

Example #2. From a press release on the Hong Kong government website announcing a movie about prehistoric sea creatures:

"Eighty million years ago, many places on Earth were *undersea*. For example, today's Kansas, in the central United States, was at the bottom of a great inland sea dividing *the then North America* into two. A *warmth* climate meant more of the globe was submerged."

Comments: *"Undersea"* is an adjective. The press release should read that places were *"under the sea."* *"The then North America"* is a poor choice of words; what the announcement is really referring to is *"modern-day North America."* The adjective that should be used here is *"warm,"* not *"warmth."* The Hong Kong government should be more careful.

* * *

Example #3. From the website of the Hong Kong and Macao Affairs Office of the Chinese State Council:

Main Functions:

The Hong Kong and Macao Affairs Office of the State Council is an organ assisting the *Premier to deal* with affairs relevant to Hong Kong and *Macao, its* main functions are as follows:

1. *Make researches* on various aspects of Hong Kong and Macao societies.

2. *Make overall planning* for and coordinate the official contacts between different mainland departments and localities on the one side and *HKSAR and MCSAR* on the other.

3. Be responsible for the working contacts with the *Chief Executives* of *HKSAR and MCSAR* as well as the governments of the two SARs.

4. Promote and coordinate *the* cooperation and exchange in the *field* of economics, science, technology, education, culture, *etc*. between the mainland and the two SARs of Hong Kong and Macao.

5. Be responsible for *examining and* approving as well as issuing travel documents for public servants going to *HK* and Macao.

6. Participate in the management of *service export to and mainland companies* in *HK* and Macao.

7. Promote the Basic Laws of *HKSAR and MCSAR*, as well as the principles and policies of the central government concerning *HK* and Macao.

Comments: A major world power like China should take the time and money to see that its translations into English (and other languages) demonstrate care and sophistication. This looks like it was written by a barely educated sixth former. Compare the changes specified below with the rules discussed earlier in the booklet:

* In the introductory paragraph, "*premier*" should not be capitalized. It should be "*in dealing with*," not "*to deal with*." There should be a period after "*Macao*," and "*its*" should be capitalized to indicate the start of a new sentence.

* "*Research*" should not be in the plural. Also, a person does not "*make research*" or "*make planning*;" a person "*conducts research*" or "*carries out planning*."

* It should be "*make overall plans*." "*HKSAR*" and "*MCSAR*" should be spelled out fully in the first reference, and both should be preceded by "*the*" (*the Hong Kong Special Administrative Region*).

* "*Chief Executives*" should not be capitalized.

* The word "*the*" should not appear before "cooperation." It should be "*fields*" (plural), since there is more than one: the *fields* of economics, science or technology.

* In point 5, remove "*examining and…*" The office doesn't examine travel documents or public servants, it issues travel documents and approves servants' trips.

* Initials like "*HK*" are fine in telephone text messages, but they should not be used in a formal document. Spell out "*Hong Kong*."

* "*Participate in the management of service export to and mainland companies…*" is an incomplete sentence and means nothing in English.

* * *

Example #4. An item from the website of the Democratic Party of Hong Kong:

40% Respondents Support *Transforming RTHK to become* the Hong Kong Public Broadcasting Corporation
11ˢᵗ June 2007

A telephone survey of 1,150 respondents was conducted by the Democratic Party *during late April - mid May.* The findings show 61.2 % respondents *believed* public service broadcasting was needed in Hong Kong, 42.2% *had a good impression over performance* of RTHK, 48.9%

supports the suggestion *of Committee* on Review of Public Service Broadcasting to set up an independent public broadcasting body, 40% *respondents support transforming RTHK* to become the Hong Kong Public Broadcasting Corporation.

The Democratic Party believes that RTHK should be transformed *to* the Hong Kong Public Broadcasting Corporation. Lawmaker Lee Wing-tat will move a motion regarding the issue *on coming Wednesday*, *by* urging the authority to expeditiously review the future role, positioning and development *direction* of RTHK, actively study the feasibility of transforming RTHK *to become* the Hong Kong Public Broadcasting Corporation, and conduct public consultation on the results of the review and the study.

Comments: A political party whose founding chairman is a U.K.-trained barrister should be ashamed of itself for publishing such terrible English.

* "*llst June*??!!" Shameful. It should be "*11ᵗʰ*" June.

* "*Transforming* RTHK *to become…*" "had a good impression *over* performance…" "*on* coming Wednesday…" "*48.9%* supports the suggestion of *Committee on Review of Public Service Broadcasting…*" Wrong verb, wrong or missing prepositions (it should be 40% *of* Respondents…), missing articles: very bad English all around. And in a list like the one above, the verb tenses have to be consistent: 61.2% *believed*, 48.9% *supported*, 40% *supported*.

* * *

Example #5. Two items from the website of the Democratic Alliance for the Betterment of Hong Kong, another Hong Kong political party:

Survey Reveals Senior Citizens Require More Support
2009.11.15

In support of the United Nation's International Day for the Elderly on 15 November, the DAB conducted a phone survey to investigate the standard of living amongst Hong Kong's elderly community. The DAB asked questions relating to health, financial situations and general living conditions.

The survey of 681 senior citizens over the age of 60 was conducted from 30 October to 5 November and *comprised of 11* questions. The

DAB Chairman Tam Yiu-chung and Deputy Spokesperson for Welfare Services Kathy Siu presented the findings at a media conference held on 15 November. From the findings, DAB discovered that ***many senior citizens are under severe financial pressure*** often avoiding visiting a doctor when they fall ill (38.3%) or not having enough money to buy food (20.3%). Also, 66.4% believe that *the government do not do enough* for Hong Kong's senior citizens…

DAB's findings also revealed that 25.3% of those who were surveyed are using the government subsidy as their main income. Many senior citizens still seek employment (10.1%) to gain extra funds for food and medical bills.

Reviewing the results from the survey, the *DAB make* the following suggestions to the government…

The government should provide transportation discounts for the elderly. *DAB suggest the government allow senior citizens to travel* at a discounted rate on *Sunday's* to enable them to visit friends and relatives…

The *DAB hope* that the government *will take action and do more* to support Hong Kong's elderly community. The findings from the survey show that many senior citizens are without adequate food and medical care, which is unacceptable in today's society.

Comments:

* The main information – what this opinion poll discovered – is buried in the middle of the second paragraph instead of appearing in the lead.

* Sloppy English: It should be "*was composed of*" instead of "*comprised of*;" the government "*does not*" do enough instead of "*do not*" do enough; "*the* DAB *suggests that* the government allow senior citizens to travel;" the DAB "*hopes*" the government will take action ("*will take action and do more*" is redundant). There are missing articles. "*Sunday's*," a plural, should not have an apostrophe.

* * *

Consumer Council Receives 31 Complaints Against Slimming Companies

2009.12.06

The Consumer Council announced on 17 September that it had received several complaints regarding false advertising for 'free' slimming programmes in Hong Kong. A total of 31 complaints were made to the Consumer Council citing dishonest sales resulting in consumers losing large amounts of money.

In fact, a victim support group was formed in July to fight back over false advertising by slimming companies. The group has lobbied politicians and met with the Consumer Council and the police, but four months later, still nothing has been done to expose these companies.

On 6 December DAB Legislative Councillor Starry Lee represented the group at a media conference at the DAB Hung Hom branch to inform the media of this growing problem. A letter was also presented to the Chairman of the Consumer Council to draw his attention to this matter…

The Consumer Council should expose the fraudulent slimming companies and help the victims obtain a refund. *The victim support group actively visit internet forums* to inform others of their ordeal. As a result, members of the group have received emails and SMSs from the slimming companies threatening to sue them. The *groups* Facebook page *was also deleted*. It was recently reported that similar slimming programmes have claimed more victims in Mainland China. The Consumer Council needs to act *now*!

Comments: This press release is supposedly reporting remarks from a press conference by Starry Lee on 6 December. But the reader doesn't even learn that a press conference took place until the third paragraph. Instead of focusing on the main point, the lead paragraph tells about something that happened three months earlier, in September, and the second paragraph tells about something that happened two months before that, in July. The DAB would be lucky if the reader even reached the third paragraph before tossing this old news aside. "*The victim support group actively visit internet forums*" is not English. It was "*the group's*" Facebook page that was deleted, not "*the groups*" page. And who deleted it? The press release doesn't explain this apparently important point. This is an excellent example of how *not* to write a press release.

* * *

Example #6. Two items from the website of the government of China:

Functions of the President

According to the *Constitute*, the president of the People's Republic of China exercises both domestic functions and powers and those in foreign affairs.

Domestic functions and powers:

Promulgating laws, appointing and removing the premier, vice premiers, state councilors, ministers of ministries and state commissions, auditor-general, and secretary-general, conferring state medals and honorary titles, *issuing order* of special amnesty, proclaiming martial law and a state of war as well as *issuing order* of mobilization, according to decisions of the NPC and its Standing Committee.

Comments: It is presumably the *Constitution*, not the "*Constitute*," the sets out the president's functions and powers. The president issues "*orders*," plural, not "*order*." The main website of the one of the world's major nations, describing the functions of the highest position in the land, should be written in better English than this.

* * *

Constitution

Adopted at the Fifth Session of the Fifth National People's Congress and promulgated for implementation by the Proclamation of the National People's Congress on December 4, 1982, and amended in accordance with the amendments to the Constitution of the People's Republic of China adopted at the First Session of the Seventh National People's Congress on April 12, 1988, at the First Session of the Eighth National People's Congress on March 29, 1993, at the Second Session of the Ninth National People's Congress on March 15, 1999, and at the Second Session of the 10th National People's Congress on March 14, 2004.

Comments: A free trip to the first session of the *next* National People's Congress to anyone who can explain what this 100-word-long sentence means.

* * *

Example #7. From the Chinese government website:

China to step up economic restructuring

Chinese Premier Wen Jiabao told *netizens* on Feb. 27, 2010 that to secure a steady and fast economic development, the most important thing is *to well treat the relationship among economic restructuring, the transformation of development pattern and inflation control*. Following are some facts about the country's economic restructuring:

China has pledged more efforts to accelerate economic restructuring this year to make its growth more sustainable, after its economy posted a strong recovery of 8.7 percent growth in 2009, exceeding its target of 8 percent...

The Political Bureau of the Communist Party of China Central Committee issued a statement Monday which vowed that *the government would accelerate economic restructuring and push forward substantive progress in changing the mode of economic development this year, while continuing the proactive fiscal policy and moderately loose monetary policy*.

The nation's top leaders have reiterated the need for economic restructuring, which analysts said would be the focus of this year's *macro policy*.

Chinese President Hu Jintao said on Feb. 3 that "on the surface, the global financial crisis impacted on the speed of China's economic growth, but in essence it was the economic growth pattern that was worst hit."

"*The transformation of economic development mode brooks no delay based on a comprehensive judgement on international and domestic economic situation*," Hu said.

The key for the transformation was to achieve it "at an accelerated speed" and with practical effects, he noted.

Comments: This is full of babble and jargon, along with a lot of plain bad English. "…the most important thing is *to well treat the relationship among economic restructuring, the transformation of development pattern and inflation control*." No lay person reading this would understand that phrase. And how does one "*well treat*" such a relationship? Does this mean someone has been "bad treating" the relationship until now?

"…*the government would accelerate economic restructuring and push forward substantive progress in changing the mode of economic development this year, while continuing the proactive fiscal policy and moderately loose monetary policy*"? Again, this is gibberish, not English.

And look at President Hu's comment: "*The transformation of economic development mode brooks no delay based on a comprehensive judgement on international and domestic economic situation*." There are missing articles in that sentence ("*the*" economic development mode, "*the*" international and domestic economic situation), and even if the articles are added, the sentence makes no sense. We assume that the Chinese president speaks quite proper Chinese; his English translators make him look uneducated.

###

APPENDIX
Answers to practice sentences

#1: Fill in the correct articles:

1. **The** former prime minister of Great Britain received **an** honorary degree from **The** University of Hong Kong in recognition of **the** work he had done to combat world hunger.

2. **A** horse, **an** elephant and **an** unidentified third animal all escaped from **the** zoo last night.

3. **An** off-duty police officer chased and caught **a** mugger who had just robbed **a** couple in **the** Kowloon section of Hong Kong last night. **The** mugger was later identified as **the** same man who had robbed **an** elderly woman **an** hour and **a** half earlier on Hong Kong Island.

4. **The** chief executive of **the** Hong Kong government was quoted today in **The** Times of London as saying **a** vote will be held in **the** Legislative Council on **the** question of universal suffrage in Hong Kong "at **the** appropriate time."

5. In **the** United States, **an** FBI agent is a federal officer.

#2: Verb tenses:

1. The weather **has been** terrible these last few days. **It's been raining** so hard our dog **would not go** outside for his regular walk.

2. I **have studied** nonstop for the past five days. I think I **will be ready** for the final exam.

3. If you **take/had taken** more time, you **will not forget/would not have forgotten** to pack your presentation materials.

4. I **moved** into this flat just last April, and now **I am moving/have moved** again.

5. My friend **has** a very dangerous job. Every time I **see** him, I'm afraid it **will be/could be/is going to be** the last.

6. I **go** to China every week for business. I almost feel as if I **am living** there.

8. I **have seen** the movie twice already, and I **am seeing/will see**) it again this evening.

9. He **had lain** down for only a few minutes before the alarm rang and he had to **get** up again.

10. I **had competed** in a dozen marathons before I **entered** the big New York Marathon last year.

11. He **laid** down the sack of cement and then **lay** down to take a short nap.

12. It took us six hours of tramping around the fields, but we finally **laid** out the boundaries of the property. I got so tired at one point that I **lay** down on a rock to rest. We plan to **lay** out the boundary of the second plot tomorrow.

13. We were ordered to **grind** the flour from 8 a.m. to 7 p.m., and once it was all **ground**, we put it in sacks and **laid** each sack on the ground outside the mill. Then we all **lay** down and immediately **fell** asleep.

###

ACKNOWLEDGMENTS

My thanks to the folks at the Journalism and Media Studies Centre for their invaluable help in getting this book published. In particular, thanks to Professor Ying Chan, the director of the JMSC, who first proposed the book and herded it through to its completion; Matthew Leung, the JMSC's creative director, who oversaw the design and editing of the book; Velentina Ma, one of my fellow journalism lecturers, who handled publicity and other outside contacts; and Pauline Ng, administration manager of the JMSC, who took care of contract matters and liaison with the distributor, Hong Kong University Press. Thanks also to Michael Duckworth, publisher of the HKUP, and Winnie Chau and Maria Yim of HKUP, for their advice and assistance in getting the book out under a tight deadline with their usual professional skill.